# HOW TO BECOME A SUCCESSFUL BETA READER BOOK 2

## MASTERING THE ART OF CRAFTING FEEDBACK

### DEDRIE MARIE

ISBN: 978-1-7327090-1-0

*For my little Nelson, whose snuggles during long days of writing make the "work" even more rewarding.*

# CONTENTS

**FREE VIDEO TRAINING**
Get the system I use to make my reading habit work for me:
www.DedrieMarie.com/start-beta-reading
Hope to see you there!
*Dedrie Marie*

# HOW TO BECOME A SUCCESSFUL BETA READER BOOK 2

# INTRODUCTION
*Welcome to the Best Gig Ever!*

∼

Growing up in Mineral Wells, Texas, everyone I knew spoke the same language—that would be Southern, y'all! It was a small community with very little diversity. Fancy yourself a chicken-fried steak? No problem. Burger or fried chicken? Sure thing. Sushi or Thai? Hell, or a salad not swimming in Ranch soup? Not a chance. Football, baseball, and track were available for the guys in school. Softball, volleyball, and track for the gals. Only little kids played soccer—well, and foreigners...on TV.

The first time I ever ate sushi was while on vacation in Antigua well into my adult years. My traveling companion and I were seated at a table at a Japanese restaurant. I didn't even know what sushi was, truth be told. He ordered it. Technically it was sashimi. And when the little slabs of oh-my-god-they-forgot-to-batter-and-fry-that stuff was placed on the table before us, my mouth gaped. I'm not exactly sure what I said, but the couple next to us got a chuckle out of it.

I love to meet new people. And anytime there's opportunity to do so, I jump on it. By the end of the night, this couple and we were having drinks, laughing, and swapping stories about food mishaps. Apparently, they were once invited to a lord's house for brunch in London. David had mistakenly covered all his breakfast items in chocolate sauce thinking it was a brown gravy of sorts. The servers behind the buffet snickered about him, and to stand his ground, David ate the entire mess and then went back for seconds, drizzled again in chocolate "gravy."

This couple had British English accents, and obviously we all spoke the same language. Yet somehow, there were more than a few moments of needed "translation." Using words familiar to you and your upbringing does not always mean someone who also uses those same words will understand you. For example, I spent a good bit of time thinking David was a man who had conquered his angry past. Why? Because he kept referring to how "pissed" he'd been when this happened and how "pissed" he'd been when that happened. To hear him laugh about it, well, I just assumed it was in the past and now something he could look back on through a lighter lens. I did finally figure out that he in fact meant he was drunk, not upset.

Similarly, David thought I was at times morbid and a bit crass. I spoke of having "a coughin' fit" at the beginning of the week. He took this to mean that I was, in my thirties, prematurely prepared for my own funeral: *having a coffin fit*. When I spoke of sitting on my fanny all day—well...you can look that one up. Just know he and his wife had a chuckle at my expense on this one. My point is, we spoke the same language yet had communication mix-ups that led me to believe that he was an angry man and him to believe that I was a vulgar and morbid woman. Of course, more context, a bit of explaining, and a lot of laughter cleared this up. But we don't have these luxuries when communicating in writing. That's why I've taken to a certain system when crafting my beta reading feedback. Misunderstandings so easily can occur in written communication, especially when that communication is any type of criticism.

My primary goal is to support authors. I have been given the gift of loving to read with the same passion that authors have for loving to write. And because of this, I want these amazing storytellers to succeed. I want more great stories out in the world to change the lives of others, just as many books have changed mine. But great stories don't magically appear on a first or second or third attempt. Writers must keep rewriting, digging deeper into their stories, chipping away all that the story is not, until they've unearthed exactly what the story is.

This is no easy task. It is daunting. And having help is the best way to get through the process. But reaching out for that help, in and of itself, is daunting and scary and a very vulnerable thing to do. I never lose sight of that fact when I'm beta reading or editing or even copyediting and proofreading. Every word I choose can have a great impact on a writer (positive or negative), both in regard to their story at hand as well as their confidence in their skills. It is in the remembrance of how words can affect others that we choose them wisely.

This book is intended to drive that concept home and give you the help you need to craft critique that will ensure a writer hears the criticism needed to improve the work while at the same time build them up. I don't believe in harsh words. I don't believe in ever telling someone they're not cut out to be a writer. I don't believe in telling someone their story just isn't good enough or their writing just isn't good enough.

I mean seriously, think about E.L. James' *Fifty Shades of Grey*. Ask around about the writing quality in that book—not the entertainment value or the story, but the writing itself—and you'll come away with a divided audience. Yet, clearly people are buying her books, and she's a dang multi-millionaire now. If she'd listened to someone who'd said your writing isn't good enough, she'd not be where she is now.

What I do believe in is supporting and helping writers

who have a dream to be published. And all I can do is give them my best, some well-informed guidance, and genuine encouragement. If this is an attitude you feel you can adopt, you'll do well in this field.

If you remember from *Book 1*, I talked about how it can be quite difficult to tell someone that their book needs an overhaul (not that all of them do, but it happens). You must be able to deliver tough information without sounding like a condescending jerk. You must be able to articulate your rationale behind this opinion and give them something to work with.

Some give praise just to keep the peace. How does this help the writer? Well, it doesn't (other than momentarily boosting a writer's ego, which could later be obliterated by harsh reader reviews). A beta reader needs to be able to provide *all* feedback, even the negative, so that the writer has the best chance possible to smooth out any snags before the manuscript hits the desktop of an editor, generating editing fees that could have been avoided—or in the hands of the general readership and is met with scathing reviews. This ability hinges on that attitude I spoke of just a bit ago. And to make sure your words and feedback are in alignment with this attitude, I've written this book on the art of crafting feedback. I hope you'll find it helpful and encouraging!

Just like *Book 1* knocked your socks off with the awesome fundamentals of fiction, *Book 2: Mastering the Art of Crafting Feedback* has some great lessons too. Here are a few:

- You'll learn of some handy-dandy tools—and how to use them—to make your beta reading life a breeze.
- You'll be given a method for combing through a book in an organized fashion, ensuring efficiency

and quality (and a means for evaluating your work production).

- You'll become a literary chameleon when you learn to read with the eyes of a reader, writer, and editor.
- You'll be the angel in disguise when you can spot and accurately recommend the appropriate editorial needs of a book.
- You'll feel like a rockstar when you learn to create an analysis and editorial letter for your author.
- And you'll be thought absolutely charming when authors experience your beta reading etiquette.

In *Book 1*, you learned the fundamentals of fiction. You now have the perfect foundation for reading with a purpose. If you somehow missed *Book 1*, you can get it here (https://www.books2read.com/u/mZP7Xe). In that book, I talked about the massive influx of self-publishing authors since Amazon changed the publishing game. There are literally millions of books self-published. Economist Claude Forthomme wrote an article in 2014 estimating the average number of books published a day. (Amazon has since removed the exact numbers listed on their site and gives vague estimations.) Broken down, the numbers came to five books every minute. That's a whole lotta folks needing author services such as beta reading, proofreading, editing, cover designing, audioproduction, etc.

I'm telling you, the captivating world of books needs you like never before. And I'm dedicated to helping book lovers turn their passion for fiction into fascinating "anywhere ya want" careers. So I think if you're serious about reading with a purpose, a purpose that benefits you, authors, and other readers, then you've found the perfect guide to set you on the path to a glorious new and exciting adventure. Since you've completed *Book 1* and are still with me, I'm gonna assume you're getting pretty serious about learning this crazy fun skill that allows you to position yourself front and center for authors.

Welcome. Now let's get to it!

**Note: Beta readers do not edit, copyedit, or proofread the work, but beta reading certainly is an excellent way to get your foot in the door and start building an author clientele, should you want to pursue offering these (and many other) potential additional author services.**

**If you find you dig that kind of work, i.e., you see the grammar issues, the typos, that extra space or contextual flaw and you feel compelled to correct it, then you may consider learning the valuable skills of copyediting and proofreading. Pretty much every work will need some level of copyediting or proofreading, but during the beta read is not the time to tackle it.**

**If you find a few areas to use as examples for your author, you can always point them out to bolster your recommendation for editing services. And if you happen to be able to personally offer those services, well, it's a win-win.**

**Check out COMMA SUTRA: Proofreading Fiction at www.DedrieMarie.com/lit-u. It's an online**

course I teach. I absolutely love to proof. I find it oddly therapeutic!

**So who is this book for?**

- those who have read *Book 1* and are passionate about fiction and want to contribute to that fiction in a real way
- anyone who feels a deep desire to help authors craft the best stories possible
- anyone who is interested in learning an effective system for beta reading and crafting meaningful, effective, and actionable feedback that is presented in a professional and helpful manner
- those who already beta read but are interested in seeing another's approach, possibly improving upon their personal practice

**Who is this book not for?**

- those who feel it doesn't take skills to be an effective beta reader
- those who felt whooped by all the reading they've done so far in this book
- those not willing to invest time and effort in their personal education
- those who don't feel they can adopt an attitude of being supportive and encouraging to a writer, even when they feel that writer's skills are lacking

Before we even start, let me tell you about some super sweet bonus materials you'll get with this guide. I'll provide you with helpful templates to use in your beta reading services, such as nondisclosure agreements, questionnaires, self-editing checklists, and project tracking. I'll list my recommendations for certain tools and services that have helped me with my beta reading business. You'll also find recommended reading that I felt helped me along my journey in learning this skill, as well as some reading that I found encouraging and relevant.

So with that said, let's get this party started!

# RECOMMENDED READING

*Thrill Me* by Benjamin Percy

I recommend *Thrill Me* by Benjamin Percy for the simple reason of getting you in the mood for seeing just how great genre writing can be. There's this whole debate out in the literary world. Some say genre fiction can't possibly be good; it's too formulaic, too many boundaries. But that's simply not true. You learned in *Book 1* of the genre conventions and reader expectations; but if you'll remember, one of those expectations was that the work would not be predictable. Benjamin Percy proves that literary and genre fiction are not mutually exclusive. Creativity can absolutely shine through, even in genre fiction. My hope is that this book will help you see how—and that you can (and should) envision such for your authors. Mr. Percy is one hell of a writer. This book is on the craft, but I promise it is every bit as entertaining as one of his novels or shorts, and it's a super quick read. I hope you enjoy!

# PART I

~

"Can I be blunt on this subject? If you don't have time to read, you don't have the time (or the tools) to write. Simple as that."

— STEPHEN KING, ON WRITING

I realize that Mr. King is speaking strictly about writing here. On page 147 in his book, *On Writing*, he talks about how, if he had a nickel for every person who wanted to be a writer but couldn't find the time to read, he could buy a steak dinner.

It makes total sense, right? How can anyone expect to grow in their craft if they don't study the successful crafters before them?

I'm sure a remarkably scant few are born with the innate ability to just belt out a great book from the genius of their mind, but I'm thinking the majority should take up reading as a study—just as any professional studies a subject or craft or skill. I hold this same philosophy true to the beta reader as well. How can we possibly expect to have a solid grasp on the Mystery genre and its long list of subgenres (which evolves over time) unless we've read the classics, the wildly successful, and the newest releases? How can a beta think they can "advise" a writer on a craft they themselves do not study? It's done, don't get me wrong. Tons of people call themselves beta readers, editors, etc., yet they do not take their role seriously. They just dole out opinions. *How very skilled*, I sneer.

Mr. King is referring to taking this seriously. And I am too. If you want to be a beta reader that truly benefits the writers you come into contact with, do yourself (and them) a favor and read, read, read. Study and gain clarity and confidence in the genre you love. Especially now that you have an understanding of what the components are of a novel, you can read to sharpen your beta senses, see what works, what doesn't, and know why.

# ONE
## SUPERQUICK REVIEW OF BOOK 1
### *Just Makin' Sure You Were Paying Attention!*

If you're anything like me, you like a snazzy refresher to bring the brain back up to speed before getting to full-speed-ahead. I'll make this short and sweet.

In *Book 1: Learning the Fundamentals of Fiction*, you learned the following:

- a beta reader is someone who reads an author's self-edited and/or professionally edited work and provides effective and actionable feedback on the overall project
- a beta reader can opt to read for free, quid pro quo, or professionally for a fee
- a broad overview of the qualities and skills needed to become an effective and valued beta reader
- how to identify standard literary elements (or lack thereof) in a manuscript and provide suggestions using said elements to improve the overall work
- how to read for authenticity, veracity, and unity of the story
- how to read for proper genre conventions to ensure the story fits the author's intended market (and help them avoid the biggest mistakes possible when launching their book)

- how to read and give feedback with the eyes of a reader, writer, and editor
- how to give authors a great experience with your beta reading etiquette

**EDITORIAL STAGES**

I'm going to walk you through, very briefly, the stages of a novel, from final drafts to being publisher-ready. This was covered in greater detail in *Book 1*, so I'm just going to list them here:

STEP 1: SELF-EDIT

This is the stage where the author sets about getting the book as close to polished as they can without too much outside help. A self-edit can be challenging. To help your authors—and provide above-and-beyond service—you can always send them a self-editing checklist. (Link available in Chapter 9.)

STEP 2: BETA READ

In this process, a beta (you!) will read the manuscript and provide feedback touching on areas of strengths and weaknesses.

STEP 3: DEVELOPMENTAL EDIT

This is the stage where an editor evaluates the manuscript and provides help with the overall story and writing.

STEP 4: LINE EDIT

A line edit focuses on the prose and its overall effect and is performed by a line editor.

STEP 5: COPY EDIT

Without altering the context, this level of editing focuses on grammar, spelling, word usage, style, punctuation, jargon, consistency and continuity, as well as inappropriate figures of speech before the work is set into type and formatted. It is performed by a copyeditor.

STEP 6: DESIGN

The cover design should be done by a professional cover designer. Period. (Najdan at Iskon Design was the super fab designer for the covers in this Lit-Lucrative series.) This is also the point when the interior design is completed. An author can invest in a professional here as well (especially if many photographs or other images are included). Or if their skill set allows, they can utilize book design templates (I love The Book Designer) or design programs (Vellum is a DIY program that is super easy to use) and proceed independently.

STEP 7: PROOFREAD

This portion of the process happens once there is an actual proof to review; that is, a typeset, formatted, and designed facsimile of a finished product. A proofreader fine-combs the work for any typos, text or formatting errors, and confirms that the work is ready for publication. (Think you may like this type of work? Check out COMMA SUTRA: Proofreading Fiction at http://www.dedriemarie.com/lit-u.)

In a very tight nutshell, that covers the editorial process of getting a manuscript ready to publish. As you can imagine, it is quite a journey for the author; and like any worthwhile investment, it can be a timely and pricey one. For these two reasons alone, you can see that a writer must place a ton of trust in the process and the people chosen to be a part of it. Make every effort to ensure their decision to trust in you is a rewarding one! In return for your great effort, you just may earn yourself a lifetime client—or better yet, a lifetime client that sends all their writerly friends knockin' on your door.

## GENRE-SPECIFIC READING

Remember, it is important to establish what genre the author intends the book to be marketed in. This will allow for a focused read with convention expectations at the heart of consideration. The easiest way to get this information is via an author questionnaire (link provided in Chapter 9). From this you can gain a sense of how the author feels about their work, what their perspective is on their strengths and weaknesses, what genre they've intended to write in, and most importantly, what story they've intended to tell.

## UNDERSTANDING THE AUTHOR'S GOAL

Understanding your author's goals is paramount to helping them write their best book possible. My primary concern in this area starts with genre; that is, what genre are they intending the story to be marketed in. Then you need to understand where this author is in the writing and editing process of the book. All this information is valuable in forming your feedback for the author. It helps you to know where to give the most focus. This information can also be gleaned from the questionnaire.

## THE JARGON

While it is not necessary to be able to scribble out feedback with the fury and wordsmith powers of an English doctorate or managing editor, it certainly will improve the articulation of your thoughts on the matter to know a word or two specific to the literary and publishing industry. You gotta be able to throw down with a little lingo, know what to say and what others are saying—and we covered a great list of words in *Book 1*. For your convenience, I've included that list at the back of this book in Appendix A.

## CREATIVE WRITING—THE BASICS

Although each genre has its own set of conventions, there is a foundation to all creative writing consisting of these literary elements: theme, setting, time, plot, character, point of view, dialogue, tone, voice, and style. All aesthetically effective works of fiction contain such elements—the building blocks, so to speak—and you learned about them in *Book 1*.

## GENRE CONVENTIONS

Conventions are the defining elements of any genre. They are the universal or agreed-upon expectations of story structure, style, and/or subject matter. Genre not only involves an author following a set of conventions to adequately categorize the work, but it also plays a huge role in reader response. We covered some of the most popular categories you'll be encountering as a beta reader and the reader expectations of those categories: Romance, Mystery/Thriller/Suspense, Horror, Science Fiction/Fantasy, Western, and Young Adult.

## BETA READING ETIQUETTE AND TIPS

- Identify the author's vision.
- Don't beta read for genres or subjects you don't enjoy.
- Be honest.

- Deliver criticism with the vehicle of praise.
- Be specific.
- Avoid negative absolutes.
- Respect deadlines and keep clear communication.
- Respect the author's guidelines.
- Hang up your personal agenda before taking on a novel.
- Watch your words.
- Remember that what you appreciate appreciates.

## BETA READER EXPECTATIONS

- Many beta readers read for hobby only. Some, who write, read in exchange for a returned beta read of their own work. Some read for a fee. Whatever the agreement, be clear up front before taking on the work. That way, you'll know what to expect from the author when the project is complete.
- An author may not agree with your feedback.
- An author may or may not comment on your services one way or another, leaving you wondering about their satisfaction. Just send a friendly request, short and sweet, asking for feedback or a testimonial on your services. Follow up in a week or two if necessary.
- Don't expect all of your suggestions to be acted upon. And remember that the author most likely is using more than one or two betas, as well as an editor, and will make decisions based more on a consensus basis.
- You shouldn't expect to adhere to unreasonable

deadlines. Be clear up front to avoid any confusion.
- You aren't expected to serve as a critique or brainstorming partner.
- Expect author autonomy; respect author autonomy.

That was the gist of *Book 1* and everything you need to keep in mind when reading with a purpose and compiling your effective feedback and letter. Now, let's dive a bit deeper into just exactly **how** to go about this task in an organized and constructive manner.

# EXERCISE PART I

~

The best way to figure this stuff out is just by diving in—well, sort of.

"Sink er swim, Sister," is what my daddy always said. And yet, I prefer to arrive to the swimmin' hole with the skills to not friggin' drown. Call me crazy, but I just don't believe in having to be fished out of a situation because the choice to dive in headfirst without some preparation was made.

Now, if after all this you find yourself terrified to "do it for real," then I might throw that daddy line at ya. But we're not gonna let that happen, right? Because you are going to be prepared, confident, and ready to tackle this fun and fascinating gig!

By now, you should be thinking about the genre(s) you wish to work in. Pick a book that you've read and loved that fits into one of the main genres mentioned in *Book 1*: Romance, Mystery/Thriller/Suspense, Horror, Science Fiction/Fantasy, Western, or Young Adult.

Keep it handy. You'll be needing it! (I recommend starting with one genre, one you absolutely love to read. Once you've done a fair share of them and feel solid in your understanding of the literary elements and conventions for it, you can expand and add another if that suits your fancy.)

[Marketing tip: The easiest way to stand out and build an author clientele is to specialize. Saying that you beta read everything is fine enough, but saying you specialize in historical fiction set during WWII is a much stronger approach to landing a client. You could become the go-to beta for WWII historical fiction writers.]

# PART II

~

"There is no easy way to train an apprentice. My two
tools are example and nagging."

— Lemony Snicket, Who Could That Be at This
Hour?

Now, that quote's not entirely true (in this case). I won't be
nagging you. But I will try my best to offer up examples of
how to use the tools that I find helpful.

There's not too much needed to beta read. You could
simply read a book, write up a letter or fill out a form of
questions, and be on your way. I do believe that's how the
majority of unpaid beta readers operate. I offer my services
as a professional service, a paid service. Because of that, I
feel I owe the author a wee bit more than an afterthought
response. So I use some of the same tools to beta read that I
use to edit. It makes the job easier, in my opinion. It's more
streamlined, organized, and I can move about the work
easily without losing sight of where I've been and where
I'm going.

You don't have to use these tools to beta read. But I share
them in case you choose to. Also, you may find ways to
improve upon my methods. That's wonderful, and I suggest
you use these tools and organizational methods as little or
extensively as fits your liking.

# TWO

TOOLS

*My Preferred Tools of the Trade*

I will be the first to tell you that I am on Team Print when it comes to reading purely for pleasure. I love to collect books, hold books, turn the pages. Even if I listen to an audiobook, I often will purchase the print copy so that I can reread certain excerpts or even read the book in its entirety at a later date. The editor in me likes to see the editing style as well.

I also find that I love to recommend and loan physical books to friends. It makes for a great excuse to meet up for fun discussions!

I never read fiction on my tablet or e-reader. (The e-reader was a thoughtful but rarely used gift.) I may occasionally read nonfiction on it, but only if it's something I need that very moment for maybe business purposes, such as a "how to" or something or other. However, for any editorial services I offer, I use either my laptop or iPad. Why? It's just more efficient and effective, I believe.

Also, please know that I have a love/hate relationship with technology and am not—I repeat: I am not a techie. In fact, I pretty much avoid tech as much as possible. I'm sure some are reading this thinking this backwoods chick should be publicly flogged, or at the very least should be forced to spend some time with a youngster. But, I do know it's necessary and can be learned. (I'll have you know that I did a Snoopy dance whenever I learned to create the images in this guide all by my bad self. For digital versions of the figures, go to www.dedriemarie.com/br-2-figures.)

Regarding this beta reading per this guide, I recommend a laptop or PC with Microsoft Word and/or a tablet with an app to mark up or annotate the work. There are various apps out there that you are welcome to use. I am sure that many of you are tech gods compared to me. But for those of you who really want the from-scratch pretend-I-just-crawled-out-from-under-a-rock kind of guidance, I've got ya covered. I personally use an HP laptop that's about eight years old (it's been so kind to me) with Windows 10 (not that I volunteered to upgrade...sneaky Windows) and subscribe to Office 365 to assure I always have the most up-to-date Word program. And then I have my iPad Mini. I used to use a full-size iPad but found I got tired of holding it for hours on end. Sucker gets heavy. I realize I could have gotten some sort of stand or whatnot, but I prefer to hold. So the Mini works perfectly for me. For the app, I use Branchfire's latest version of iAnnotate. It's a one-time purchase; and once you get acquainted with it, it's easy peasy lemon squeezy to use.

The author can send you their manuscript however works best for you guys: email, Google Docs, iCloud Drive, Box, Dropbox, One Drive, snail mail with a thumb drive stashed away in a bubble wrap envelope for you nostalgistas out there.

**A note regarding Google Docs: I don't recommend marking up directly in Google Docs, as handy as this may seem, especially if multiple people have access to the document. Remember, many writers use multiple beta readers and may allow all of them permission to access the file. The document will begin to look like a cluttered mess if each**

reader is marking up the same document, and reading the comments of others can inadvertently influence the feedback of someone else (you).

I always download the doc and work privately and then return it separately. Obviously, author preference can come into play here. But it's your business and you can handle things as you dang-well please; I certainly do.

You can then download it and save it to your computer or tablet. Like I said, I beta read with either Word's Track Changes or iAnnotate. With Track Changes, you can highlight and comment directly in the Word document and perform searches via the Navigation tool. To use the app on your tablet, you will need to open the file and then copy it to iAnnotate where you can mark up directly on the document using created stamps, the highlighter, typing tool, etc. There are search functions as well. We will cover the particulars of using these tools in a bit. For now, I will say that I prefer the Track Changes feature to marking up on my iPad for efficiency; but for portability (like if I decided to lounge by the pool with a manuscript, read while traveling on a plane, "work" while resting in my tent at night while camping) the iPad sure is nice.

I used to also keep a notebook and pencil handy for jotting down fleeting thoughts, questions, and notes. I just couldn't help myself; I apparently love pen and paper. Over time, as with any new skill set, I became more comfortable and efficient and no longer needed anything other than my chosen device. Obviously if you prefer to be 100 percent digital, you can use the notes feature on your tablet or create notes in your computer. Whatever floats your boat, honey.

We live in a digital age, but if you find an author that prefers to send you a hardcopy version of their manuscript (and you have the odd desire to play along), I suppose all you will need is a red pencil or pen, some sticky notes, a highlighter, a notebook, and possibly a stiff drink. I don't recommend reading this way, as nostalgic as it sounds, as it can be quite time consuming. I guarantee you will find yourself on a wild and frantic page-flipping hunt if you need to reference something previously mentioned in the manuscript and then can't find it. Picture loose pages... everywhere! Um. Hell. No.

While I did not write this book to teach tech skills (I'm laughing on the inside just reading that), I know that you may need a push in the right direction. So I've included some step-by-step guidance for getting started with both a computer running Windows and an iPad using iAnnotate.

## TRACK CHANGES

Typically, an author's manuscript will change hands a few times before it makes its way to the publishing stage. As it moves through the editing stages, lots of changes will undoubtedly be made. The handiest-dandiest way to track these changes is with Microsoft Word's Track Changes feature.

Track Changes allows the author to review suggested changes, such as additions and deletions, including any comments, questions, and recommendations. After the changes and comments have been reviewed, the author will accept or reject them and create a new, fresh manuscript for the next phases of the editorial process. A good practice (for the author) is to keep a copy of each stage of changes. By simply renaming the document (Draft 1, Draft 2, Beta 1, Draft 3, Edit 1...you get the idea) each time it's touched by another set of hands or revised, the author can later go back and get an overview of how their book blossomed from the original clunky draft to the final awesomeness that it has become!

## PREPARING TO RECEIVE AND MANAGE FILES

There are quite a few different ways to receive a manuscript from an author. The two most used options are via email and Google Docs. However they choose to send the file, you'll need to download it onto your computer and save it in a folder you've created specifically for this work. Be sure to name it something that will be easily referenced later. I typically assign each author a folder and make subfolders for each of their projects which houses the manuscript and any related documents: NDA, question-naire, worksheets, etc. Once saved, you can open the file (if you haven't already) and turn on Track Changes.

To use Track Changes, you will first need to enable it. This is important! For beta reading, it's probably a no-brainer. When I am copyediting or proofing, I've caught myself a few pages in before I realized I was making hard changes to the document rather than working in Track Changes which features my *suggested* changes. I had to undo everything, turn the feature on, and then start again. Doh!

Before I get too deep here, I need to make it clear that I'm working in Word on a system that runs Windows. This can easily be done on a Mac, but the layout is a touch differ-ent. My mother, who's less of a techie than I, was able to follow these instructions using her Mac and figured it out, no problemo. To you Mac users, if you get stuck with any of this, just ask Uncle Google or Aunt YouTube. They love you and have all the answers.

## USING THE FEATURES

To turn the feature on, you'll need to have a Word document open. Now open the **Review** tab in Word's ribbon (that horizontal bar of control options across the top of the document) and click on **Track Changes.** Then select the type of markup. The default is the **Simple Markup.** You will change this to **All Markup** located in the dropdown menu. **All Markup** shows all edits with a different color of text and a line leading to the right margin with notations of any actions made.

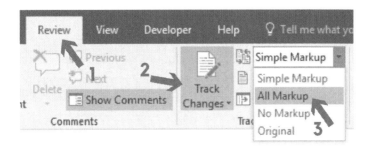

*fig. 2.1*

Once this feature is turned on, anything added, deleted, highlighted, or commented on will appear in the inline text as well as the right margin of the page. These are presented in four categories: formatted, deleted, inserted, or comment. As a beta reader, most of your dealings will be in the form of comments. Remember, you are not copyediting or proofreading; so don't get change happy here.

Just so you'll be informed, know that deleting and

adding text will appear in line with a notation out in the right margin. Any formatting changes (indents, style changes, spacing, font, etc.) will also be displayed in this margin. This draws the author's attention to any suggestions made.

But as I said, it's the highlight and comment features that we'll most be using. This is how you bring awareness to specific areas, make suggestions, and ask specific questions. This is done by selecting a word or portion of text, then activating the comments feature by clicking **New Comment** in the **Review** tab in your Word ribbon. This will open up a comment bubble in the right margin, and you can type in whatever suggestion, comment, or question you have.

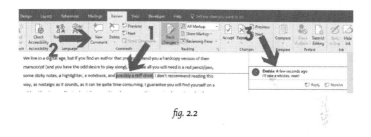

*fig. 2.2*

If you've made a comment and wish to delete it—maybe your question has been answered in the next few pages— then simply hover your cursor over the comment, right click, and select **Delete Comment**. Gone, lickety-split!

## ACCEPTING OR REJECTING EDITS AND COMMENTS

Ultimately, this final call on what to keep and what to dismiss is up to the author. It's their book after all. But it's important that you know how to do this as well in case you find yourself in the position of educating your author who is unfamiliar with Track Changes.

Once they have carefully reviewed your markups and comments, they will then go through each of them one by one to either accept or reject it. For inline markups, the author will right click over the text and choose to either accept or reject the edit from a dropdown menu. To address comments, once they've read the comment, they will click on the comment and then, from the **Review** tab in the ribbon, they will select the **Delete** feature and then **Delete** from the dropdown menu. The comment will then be removed.

This is the one-by-one method which I recommend so that no comment goes unaddressed. Beta readers and editors have put much thought into their edits and suggestions, and it would be the best practice for the author to go through each, one by one, and give it great consideration before taking action to either accept, reject, or delete. If they've opted to read and address all comments and feel comfortable deleting all at once, they can elect to do so in the same dropdown by choosing **Delete All Comments in Document**. (The same idea goes for accepting or rejecting inline changes—they have the option to **Accept All** or **Reject All** from the respective dropdown menus.)

*fig. 2.3*

**FIND OR NAVIGATION**

The other feature that will come in handy while beta reading is the Find or Navigation feature. Say you've made your way through a story, pluggin' right along, and then it hits you: *I thought Philomena's horrible father shaved her head to punish her when she was seen twirling her hair around her finger, flirting with Mr. Jenkins. How did she just tuck it behind her ear?* Or *I could have sworn Jeffrey's sword was confiscated in the night while he lay passed out after a good tavern brawl. How did he just wield that sucker at Fat Tim Wimberly? Did he get it back? When?* For these instances, you can do a quick search and find that scene to review for discrepancies.

It's super simple. Here's how. In your Word ribbon, select **Home**. To the far right, you will see options in an **Editing** feature. Select the top one: **Find**. This will open a Navigation feature to the left of the document. In the search box, simply type the word(s) that you feel will get you to the scene needed to research your question. It will pull up all instances of that word throughout the book. You can also type in phrases to get more specific, but they have to be accurate. Then you can simply click the down arrow below that search box to view each instance, which you will see highlighted in the document.

Here's an easy example: I'm reading along what I've written in this guide and it hits me that I've called it *Track* Changes and *Tracked* Changes. Maybe I should check this out. (This can be like checking name consistency in a story —you know, Jolene, Joleene, Jolean, Joleeeene...if you've now got Dolly Parton stuck in your head, you're welcome.)

Here's what it will look like. See the words *Tracked Changes* highlighted in yellow and circled?

*fig. 2.4*

That's Track Changes in a neat, sweet nutshell!

These are obviously nowhere near all the features of Word's Track Changes, but they are the primary tools you will use when beta reading, compiling your comments, and preparing your analysis. In Chapter 5, I will show you how to use these features to quickly compile all your handy-dandy comments and input them into one consolidated, easy-to-view place.

## IANNOTATE

There are a multitude of various annotation apps out there that will allow you to mark up documents on your tablet. Obviously, you can choose whichever application floats your boat and gets the job done. Like I said, I'm no techie, but I've managed to find an app that's super afford-able, offers lots of features (of which I use like three...I kid), can work with various file types, and allows me to share the marked-up and completed file easily for the author's review. (Also, if you ever need to add your signature to a document, such as in a contract/agreement, and don't want to print, sign, scan, email, whatever, this comes in handy.)

So I mentioned lots of features. To give you an idea just how disinterested in technology I am, here's a quick story:

When the new Nissan Juke came out, I had to have one. Why? Who knows. Maybe the fact that looking at it head on reminded me of a snarling ogre. I did name mine Funky Fiona after all (for you Shrek fans). But that's beside the point. Anyways, I hunted one down in Houston, Texas, that had the features I wanted: leather seats, navigation, turbo engine, and a beautiful gunmetal gray finish. This car had a push-button start. When I got ready to drive off the lot, I had to march back in and ask how to start the damn thing. (Note: When I test drove, the car was already running.) Apparently, you have to depress the brake before pushing the start button. Okay, whatevs.

After having this thing for about four months, someone asked me, "What's this button on the handle for?"

"I don't know."

"Like, you've never noticed it?"

"Yeah, I've noticed. I just haven't looked into it."

I'll wrap this up. I had no interest in these buttons. My friend did. So I handed over the keys and went inside while he tinkered with the fob and buttons. He later informed me that I had something called smart entry or whatever and that I didn't need to use my keys or fob to unlock the car. I could merely just push the button on the door handle while having the keys on my person. It was just as quick to get in the car now as if it were never locked.

"Well, hell! Okay, thanks!"

My friend looked at me sideways. "I can't believe you never wanted to figure that out. It's your *new* car."

"Eh," I shrugged.

I also traded in this car a few years later having never set the radio stations. Tech just ain't my thang.

What I'm trying to say is that I will make sure you can get the job done with this app. And I promise that, if I can do it, you can do it. But you may one day feel the urge to shoot me a message teaching me just how much more that app can do. And if you do, I'll happily thank you and offer up a virtual high five. For now, just know you'll learn all you need to beta a book. Now back to iAnnotate.

At the time of this writing, the iAnnotate app costs $9.99 (a one-time purchase...yay!), has a 4/5-star rating, and is age rated at four-plus years old. So if you struggle, you can always give yourself a giggle by remembering that four-year-olds have mastered this app. You're welcome.

Simply purchase and download the app from the app store. (Note: This application is for Apple devices only, hence the cute little "i" glued before "Annotate." Branchfire is currently working on an Android version to be released sometime in 2018, they say. It's getting pretty far into the year, so I wouldn't hold your breath.) This is the iAnnotate icon you're looking for.

**SETTING UP IANNOTATE**

Once downloaded and opened, you'll be asked how you wish to work in the app, for example, within iCloud or Dropbox or in your device. Choose which option works best for you. You can always change it and/or add more options later. If you are unsure and just ready to get this show on the road, choose **On This Device**. (Choosing the other options means your work is always saved in whatever storage option you choose and will be accessible from other devices, which can be handy and is a nice safeguard against device crashes and whatnot.)

*fig. 2.5*

It will then tell you that your files will be auto backed up and stored on this device as Local Files. Tap "set up now" to complete this step. Next you'll be presented with a Quick Reference Guide. It's about fourteen pages with little snap-shots of all the features this app offers. I would read through it as it has great visual aids.

**CREATING TOOLBARS**

(I've included bulleted step-by-step instructions for creating the toolbars following this explanation.)

You'll see a **red pencil icon** in the top right corner of your screen. This opens and closes a preset toolbar that hangs out to the right of your document. This toolbar will be where you work from. It's how you make your notes, highlight passages, and bookmark sections for easy navigation.

Tap the pencil again if you want that toolbar hidden. Ta da.

This toolbar is easily customizable, and you can have multiple toolbars. You can move between toolbars by tapping the **stacked-pages icon** at the very bottom of the toolbar. It will open your toolbars up side by side. Simple, yes?

Your next step is to set up your beta reading toolbar. Whoop! Getting closer!

At the very top of the toolbar, you'll see a **toolbox icon.**

*fig. 2.6*

Tap it to open and view all the snazzy options to choose from for your customized toolbar. They are grouped by function (see those tabs across the top of the box?), or you can select **All Tools** to see the whole shebang (top right tab). When the **All Tools** tab is selected, you will need to scroll down to be able to view them all.

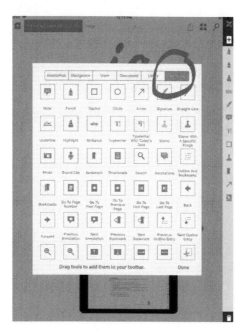

*fig. 2.7*

Don't select anything just yet. Slow your roll, Nelly. You're just window-shopping at this point. I suggest reading through what I recommend before setting yours up. Then you can decide from there if you want to stick with what I recommend or dance to the beat of your own drum.

At the top of the toolbar (vertical bar on the right of your screen) tap the **white plus-sign box** located just under the **X.** Then select **New Custom Toolbar.**

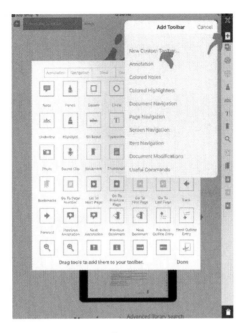

*fig. 2.8*

This will open a blank toolbar, ready for you to drag your favorite tools for beta reading right over into it. And it's super simple. Just touch and hold your finger on the tool you want and drag it to your blank toolbar. You have enough slots in one toolbar for fourteen tools. You can drag them within the toolbar to rearrange their order, as well as pull them out of your toolbar and back into the toolbox (by pulling the unwanted tool straight down the toolbar until it disappears) should you change your mind.

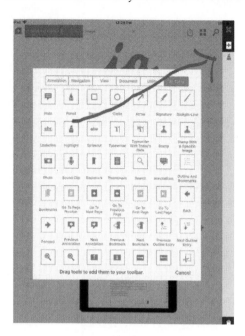

*fig. 2.9*

Once you've made your selection, you'll tap the **X** at the very top of the bar to save your new toolbar.

I know ya got ants in ya pants to get this set up...hold up for just a bit longer. I'm almost finished with my spiel.

For beta reading I use two toolbars. Toolbar 1/2 is more of my navigation toolbar and has the following tools in this order from top to bottom: **Search, Set Mark, Return to Mark, Go to First Page, Go to Last Page, Previous Bookmark, Next Bookmark, Bookmarks, Previous Annotation, Next Annotation, Go to Page Number, Add Page After, Email PDF Summary,** and **Delete Annotations on Page.** Go ahead and get this one set up and saved.

No, for real. I'm ready.

Okay, got it? Yeah? Thumbs up, you nerd!

All right. Toolbar 2/2 is my working toolbar. I create it a

bit differently. Tap the **toolbox** at the top of your toolbar. Then tap the **white plus-sign box** (second from very top). You'll get your **Add Toolbar** window again. This time select the option named **Colored Highlighters**. A partial toolbar will be created with six different highlighters in place. From here, go ahead and add the **Typewriter, Underline, Note** (not to be confused with Notes), **Bookmark, Pencil, Set Mark** (again), and **Return to Mark** (again). Tap the big **X** to save your second toolbar, and you're all set. Here's how it should look.

*fig. 2.10*

All righty, you badass super techie beta reading rockstar, go ahead and load up your toolbar as I have mine with these tools. You can always change them later to better fit your preferences.

**A quick review of those steps:**

- tap the red pencil icon
- tap the toolbox icon
- open the All Tools tab in the window
- tap the white plus-sign box at top of toolbar
- select New Custom Toolbar from the dropdown menu
- touch, hold, and drag the following tools (or whatever tools you prefer): Search, Set Mark, Return to Mark, Go to First Page, Go to Last Page, Previous Bookmark, Next Bookmark, Bookmarks, Previous Annotation, Next Annotation, Go to Page Number, Add Page After, Email PDF Summary, and Delete Annotations on Page
- tap the X at the top of the toolbar to save Toolbar 1/2
- create Toolbar 2/2 by tapping toolbox icon
- tap white plus-sign box at top of toolbar
- select Colored Highlighter from the dropdown menu
- add the following tools to the toolbar by dragging the following to it: Typewriter, Underline, Note, Bookmark, Pencil, Set Mark, and Return to Mark
- tap the X at the top of the toolbar to save Toolbar 2/2
- tap the stacked-pages icon at the bottom of the toolbar to switch back and forth between 1/2 and 2/2

Got it? Super. Now practice time.

## USING THE FEATURES

Let's use the Quick Reference Guide that came with your app as "scratch paper" to practice with. Start with the highlighter tool. There are a few ways to go about highlighting.

## HIGHLIGHTING

First, select the word "Learn" on the cover page of the guide by holding your finger on the word until it lights up in selection mode. This will pull up a black horizontal toolbar (not customizable). From this toolbar, you can choose a few options (some that we haven't selected for our custom ones). Tap **Highlight** on that bar. You will see that your selected text is now highlighted with the standard yellow. You will also see at the top of your screen options to customize that highlighting. Tap the yellow square. Viola. You now have the option to change your highlighting color. Once selected, tap the checkmark in the top right corner of the screen. Your highlighting is done.

Now tap the word "Learn" again. You'll see some options pop up again at the top. To remove the highlighting, tap the trash can and select **Delete**. Looka there. Like it was never touched.

The other two ways to highlight are with the highlighter tools in your custom toolbar. Select the text, and instead of using the black horizontal toolbar, you can tap a highlighter in your custom toolbar. Or tap a highlighter tool first and then apply it to whatever text you want in the document. This method allows for quick selections of a particular color instead of changing the color within that top customizable window each time. Fiddle with these highlighting options a bit until you get the hang of it.

. . .

## UNDERLINING

These same methods apply to Underlining. Well, that was easy now, wasn't it?

## TYPEWRITER

Tap on the **Typewriter** tool in your toolbar to open the function. You'll see options at the top to customize the font color, type, and size. To type with the tool, simply touch anywhere on the document. You'll see a box appear as well as additional options in the top customizable window. Go ahead and type a few words—say, *Dedrie is the best*—in the box. Tap the checkmark at the top right corner of the screen. And you now have annotated the document.

To adjust/edit the annotation, tap it. In that top window, select the first option (the typewriter), and now you can edit what's in the annotation box. Now tap the handler icon in that top box. It's the square with arrows around the corner. The annotation you placed on the document is now surrounded with a blinking square. Drag this square to another location on the page. Now tap the checkmark (top right). It is set. Tap your annotation once more. Tap the trash can in the top window. Select **Delete**. It is gone.

Go ahead and experiment with the Highlighters, Pencil, Underline, Bookmark, and Note tools. They should be fairly self-explanatory (especially after just mastering the high-lighter tools, you smart muthatrucka).

I will not break down every feature of this app. I'm here to teach beta reading, not app mastery. Jeez. (I kid.) But if you find you need more help, you can scroll to the bottom of the Quick Reference Guide and use the link they've imbedded. It will send you to iannotate.com. Their Support Tab will get you on your way to some helpful articles and FAQs. And you can always hit up their team via email or FB messenger. They're super helpful and respond quickly.

## OPENING A DOCUMENT WITH IANNOTATE

There are various ways to store and organize your work, should you decide to strictly work with the iPad. You can use a cloud service, Google Docs, Dropbox, etc., or create files in your iPad under the Files icon. However you choose to organize your work, be sure to create a system that houses all related documents for each author and their projects. I typically give each author a folder and create a subfolder for each project that holds any related documents such as questionnaires, NDAs, etc. Once saved, you can open the file with iAnnotate and begin working.

## USING PEN AND PAPER

To mark up and comment in this fashion, first get that stiff drink I mentioned.

That's it. *Wink*.

# THREE
## GETTING ORGANIZED
### *'Cause Wingin' It Just Won't Do!*

## PREPARING TO RECEIVE AND MANAGE FILES

As I mentioned before, the two most used methods of sending manuscripts are via email and Google Docs. Download the file onto your computer or tablet and save it in a folder you've created specifically for this work. Be sure to name the actual file something that will be easily referenced later. I typically use the author's name, project name, and pass number. So if this is my first time working with Winston Wigglesworth, I'll name the file WIGGLESWORTH, WINSTON_HIS NOVEL'S NAME_-BETA 1. If this author did a rewrite after the first round of beta reading and wants another read, I'll name it the same but with BETA 2. You get the idea?

I'm a tad bit Type-A and have my computer fairly organized. My suggestion for you is to start off as organized as possible. Create a main folder entitled BETA READING. Within that folder, create a subfolder entitled [2018] (or whatever year is appropriate). Within that folder, create a subfolder entitled [AUTHOR LAST NAME, FIRST NAME]. So each of your authors will have their own folder. And then within that folder, you'll save that author's work. Hopefully, after seeing how amazing you are at this beta reading stuff, they'll send you their next book, and the next, and the next. And then this smart little author will share your name with all his/her writing buddies, and they'll send you work. Before you know it, you've got all kinds of files.

I say, set up your system for success. Set it up like you'll have years of work with hundreds of stories. (Whether you choose to set this up in your hard drive or some other storage option is up to you. Just make sure it's easily accessible and user friendly. You'll thank yourself later!)

## TRACKING TIME

Once you have the manuscript in hand, downloaded, and ready to analyze and read, make note of the date and time the document was received, as well as the due date the feedback is required back to the writer. Then shoot the author a quick "received" message. I am a stickler about tracking my time and adhering to deadlines, and you should be too, unless your goal is to rub a whole buncha folks the wrong way. It may take some practice to form the important habit of tracking your time (you most likely will have many starts and stops), but it will serve as an effective tool for tracking your work efficiency as well as the flow of the manuscript itself.

I like to provide the author an itemized analysis of my work which includes much data from my time-tracking worksheet. I am a big cheerleader of justifying time spent on a project, especially when my work comes at a price. When an author receives just a basic Q & A worksheet, like so many do, it barely touches the surface of how much thought was put into the work (never mind the hours)—or worse, illuminates why so many betas work for free. So I began using a chart to track my efforts. This includes the time spent on each chapter, any research work, sketches, and time spent writing up the analysis/letter. It shows value, but more importantly, it serves as a tool to track data in my business such as productivity and helps immensely to set proper rates.

When freelancing, you have the perk of working when you want at any rate you set. The downside? A freelancer has to be diligent about the productivity. There's no one to keep you mindful of this, no time clock. It's just you. And it's way too easy to spread a project out far longer than necessary, driving down your wages, or worse, not realizing the true value of your work and underpricing your services. You don't have to use this example, this table, but you do need to implement a way to track your productivity, especially if you're going to be working for a fee.

I created a few tables and worksheets to simplify the beta reading process and keep me focused until finally settling into my groove. Some of these also served as a reminder to actually track my time. I can't tell you how easy it is to spend an hour or whatever reading and notating, get up and throw a load in the laundry, take my dog out, return an email or two, and then come back to pick back up where I left off. Do this a few times over a few days and you'll likely have little understanding of how much time you actually spent with the project. (Ideally, you would have large uninterrupted blocks of time to read.)

This may be no biggie for some, but I prefer to treat my beta reading as professionally as I would any of my editorial projects and therefore track it as such. (That can sometimes be a bit of a challenge as it's so much damn fun and easy to lose yourself in the story. I mean seriously, can you believe you are about to learn some super fly skills that can get you paid to read? Pinch yourself. Okay...back to business.) I find tracking is important for an accurate analysis as well. Once you get into the habit of always noting when you begin and end sessions, you may not need this tool to serve as a reminder. I now track my time directly onto the document with notations in the form of timestamps and just add them up at the end; however, I still transfer them to the time-tracking portion of the analysis sheet to reflect reading flow chapter by chapter.

This is an example of what my tracking looks like using a table. You can set yours up however works best for you.

| Project | Novel |
|---|---|
| Genre | Young Adult Fantasy Fiction |
| Received | 01-01-01 at 2:00 p.m. CST |
| Deadline | 02-01-01 |
| Confirmed Receipt | 01-01-01 at 4:00 p.m. CST |
| Returned | 01-15-01 at 12:00 p.m. CST |
| Title | Title: Subtitle (1st in series of planned 5) |
| Pages | 154 |
| Word count | 67,441 |
| Chapters | 20 |
| True Read | 3.75 hours (start: 6:00 a.m. end: 9:45 p.m.) |
| Professional Read | 2.5 hours |
| Research | .75 (included map sketch) |
| Editorial analysis and letter | 1.00 hours |
| Fee | Monthly retainer |

| Highlighting Key |
|---|
| Red: setting |
| Blue: timeline |
| Light green: main character (use the name) |
| Dark green: antagonist (use the name) |
| Purple: POV |
| Gray: theme |
| Orange: items researched |
| (Use as many as you need, especially for characters.) |

| Time spent working in sections/chapters | Pages | Time Spent (minutes) | Comments |
|---|---|---|---|
| Chapter 1 | 4 | 20 | Intro to main character, Smelty; noting time, setting, and varied species; plot established |
| Chapter 2 | 4.5 | 20 | Intro to sidekick, Rayceen; setting elaborated |
| Chapter 3 | 6 | 25 | Journey begins; confusing fight scene |
| Chapter 4 | 10 | 30 | First hurdle success; new obstacle presented with intro of second protag; rushed narrative |
| Chapter 5 | 12 | 60 | long narratives; convert to scenes; more setting revealed; additional character, Leonard, added to group; good hook established |

| | | | |
|---|---|---|---|
| Chapter 6 | 8.5 | 15 | Additional setting revealed; good opportunity for Smelty's character dev; Bar scene; sleeping together scene (potential for moral lessons, internal conflict) |
| Chapter 7 | 10 | 20 | Smelty's narrative could use dev edit; great hook at end to keep reader engaged |
| Chapter 8 | 8 | 15 | Contextual flaws; external conflict (good action scene) expand upon day 5 |
| Chapters 9 | 8 | 10 | Excellent hook to end Chapter 9 |
| Chapter 10 | 9 | 12 | Good continued momentum |

| | | | |
|---|---|---|---|
| Chapters 11 | 8 | 30 | Day 8 is three sentences long. Needed? Maybe add to it? Singing tree is excellent! |
| Chapter 12 | 5 | 25 | Good transition from 12 to 13 |
| Chapter 13 | 7 | 12 | Intro to new species and additional villain, Gregor |
| Chapter 14 | 8 | 13 | Good flow; group gets captured |
| Chapter 15 | 9 | 14 | Climatic fight scene |
| Chapter 16 | 11 | 20 | Group prevails, captures Gregor; Day 10, 11, 12 |
| Chapter 17 | 6 | 12 | Main threat revealed |
| Chapter 18 | 5 | 10 | Group reaches destiny |
| Chapter 19 | 13 | 12 | Smelty learns about self |
| Chapter 20 | 5 | 2 | Great hook to set up for the second book in the series |
| TOTALS | 154 | 377 | |

As you can see, I chose to list each chapter separately. In the past, I have also grouped my chapters according to reading sessions. However you choose, just be sure to keep good notes of each chapter's flow. I jot down key notes in the comments to help me remember why I may have spent so long in a chapter or even to serve as a little reminder of something I want to revisit or focus on in my letter.

In this example, I spent a good amount of time in the beginning chapters as there were many character types (species) introduced, as well as specific characters to get to know. You will find that keeping notes (in the manuscript) on characters' traits will serve you well when you are struck with a possible flaw later on and need to research far back into the book. In this book, the setting of a fantasy world was described geographically. To assure an accurate reflection of that world throughout the book, I spent time mapping out the setting. I literally sketched a map to determine if it made sense contextually and referred to it and added to it each time the characters moved about the world. That takes time but will save the author the heartache of finding out their readers put the book down because of a distracting setting flaw. Obviously, you don't have to be an artist, but as long as you have a map (if setting plays a significant role in the story), you can easily verify if something is logical or possibly needs tweaking.

This same premise can be used for tracking time in a story. Say the main character sets out to complete some mission by the seven-day deadline. Then you come upon a scene where the character wakes up and is going about his business on day twelve...and the story's still truckin' along. There's a problem here, right? Tracking these days will help to assure that the timeline is accurate. It's little things, but they matter bigtime.

How I use (fill out) this table varies. I've printed it—in the beginning I was married to paper and felt uncomfortable digitizing every step of the process—and kept it handy along with a notebook and pen. Now, depending on if I'm working on my computer or iPad, I'll either have it pulled up in another window to "edit" along the way, or as another document in iAnnotate and just mark it up as I go. Whatever you are most comfortable with is what you should do. And that will likely change as you get into your groove. (For the specific example of tracking time/days, you can also always just notate a timestamp at each beginning and ending point on the manuscript in a comment bubble; for instance, each time a new day is mentioned, you'd time-stamp DAY 1, DAY 2, etc., in a comment. Whatever's clever, my friend.)

## PREPARING FOR THE BETA READ

(This is the point where having that questionnaire is important. There's a link provided in Chapter 9.)

From the questionnaire, you will have an idea of where the manuscript is in the editorial process, if it's part of a series or not, what genre it's intended to fall under, what specifically the author is expecting from you (if not just a standard overall beta read—maybe they just want your opinion for editing recommendations), what the author perceives their strengths and weaknesses to be, and specific elements to focus on or ignore. This will serve as an excellent guide for how to approach the project.

If someone specifically says to focus on a certain character's development and you give them a mere one-liner on the matter, they just might feel they've wasted their time with you. If they specifically say that their manuscript is in the very beginning stages and to ignore any typos or copyediting issues (obviously point out critical contextual flaws if necessary), then don't spend a paragraph in your analysis pitching the need to hire a copyeditor. You get the gist, yes?

This may come across like a broken record and I cannot stress this enough, but correct genre labeling is vital to marketing and selling successfully. A great book in the wrong category will not sell. What it will do is tick off readers expecting something else. Ticked off readers leave ugly reviews. Ugly reviews kill future sales. So be very mindful of genre and categories and keywords while reading. I recommend poking around in the Amazon Kindle store to get a firm grasp on what books are listed in the categories and subcategories that author has assigned to it.

As an example, in the Kindle store I clicked on Romance>Paranormal>Angels. The best seller for this search on that day at that very minute was *Hotbloods 8: Stargazers* by Bella Forrest. It appears that Bella Forrest self-publishes under Nightlight Press and has produced around one hundred books (most in series). (See what I mean about there being tons of work out there?! This is just one author!) Here is her description or blurb for the **first** book in the series (Book 8 says very little, as she assumes her readers are committed by that point—not too much selling needed.)

VAMPIRES HAVE NEVER BEEN SO HOT... MILLION-BEST-SELLING AUTHOR BELLA FORREST RETURNS WITH AN ALL-NEW PARANORMAL ROMANCE!

ONE LAST ADVENTURE. THAT'S ALL RILEY WANTS BEFORE HEADING OFF TO COLLEGE AND PARTING WAYS WITH HER TWO BEST FRIENDS. SPENDING THEIR LAST SUMMER TOGETHER ON A TEXAS FARM IN THE MIDDLE OF NOWHERE ISN'T QUITE AS EXCITING AS THEY'D PLANNED...

THAT IS, UNTIL THEY STUMBLE UPON SECRETS NO HUMAN SHOULD KNOW.

MEN WHO APPEAR AND DISAPPEAR.

A GIANT WING HIDDEN IN THE CREEK.

SCREAMS IN THE DEAD OF NIGHT.

EVERY ODDITY SEEMS CONNECTED TO THEIR STRANGE—AND ALARMINGLY ATTRACTIVE—NEW NEIGHBORS, LED BY THE STORMY-EYED NAVAN. FOR REASONS SHE CAN'T EXPLAIN, RILEY FEELS DRAWN TO HIM AND THE STORY OF HIS PAST.

BUT NAVAN HAS A MONSTROUS SIDE, ONE THAT GRANTS HIM INCREDIBLE POWERS THAT ARE NOT OF THIS WORLD...AND ASHEN SKIN THAT FEELS LIKE FIRE TO THE TOUCH.

WHEN EVENTS TAKE A DANGEROUS TWIST, RILEY IS DETERMINED TO PROTECT HER FRIENDS AT ALL COSTS, BUT AS SHE UNRAVELS EACH THREAD OF THE MYSTERY, SHE FINDS HERSELF ENTANGLED IN A SUPERNATURAL CONQUEST THAT IS FAR BIGGER THAN TEXAS... AND EVEN EARTH ITSELF.

A MYSTERY.

A ROMANCE.

AND A JOURNEY THAT COULD CHANGE THE FATE OF THE HUMAN RACE.

PREPARE FOR A UNIQUE SPIN ON THE LORE YOU LOVE—AND AN ADVENTURE THAT IS AS THRILLING AS IT IS UNEXPECTED.

Here are the listed categories for this series:

Kindle eBooks > Romance > Paranormal > Angels

Kindle eBooks > Romance > Paranormal > Ghosts

Kindle eBooks > Romance > Paranormal > Vampires

## EXERCISE PART II

~

To get your head around this concept, grab that book or series of books you chose at the start of this guide. If you haven't done this yet, hop to it. Make sure it's in a genre that you enjoy.

Look it up on Amazon and check out the blurb and the category tags. Better yet, look up multiple books that you've read and see how well the information fits the story.

Reread your book, noting elements that support the blurb and category tags. (This may be a bit easier to do after finishing *Book 1* of this series. You've been given these literary elements and reader expectations in *The Fundamentals of Fiction*, but maybe after reading Chapter 4 of this book, you'll have an easier time seeing how to identify them and track them.)

# PART II RECAP

In this section you have learned about

- some helpful tools for your badass beta reading venture and how to use them:

> PC or desktop with Microsoft Word—Track Changes
> Tablet with an annotation app
> Notebook
> Pen/Pencil/highlighter/sticky notes (if reading hard copy)

- some tips for getting off to an organized and smooth sailin' start
- how to get your mindset in beta reading mode by using a book of your choice to serve as your reference example throughout the rest of this guide

# PART II RECOMMENDED READING

*How to Win Friends and Influence People in the Digital Age* by
Dale Carnegie

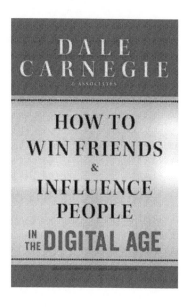

I recommend *How to Win Friends and Influence People in the Digital Age* by Dale Carnegie to get you into the mindset of communication. One of the perks of any editorial career is the nice and comfy little safety zone you get to sit in behind the computer. Rarely any meetings. Rarely even having to speak to a client. That is also one of the detriments. Our digital age has bred more ill-mannered folks than ever before. We have the right to free speech, thank goodness; but that somehow has turned into the assumption that we should speak what's on our minds with little regard for those on the receiving end. I'm not in the business of kissing bootay. I don't sugarcoat. But I know firsthand that how you communicate, especially in writing, can make or break relationships and networks. I think we all could use a refresher on how to deal with others. And this book offers some really great strategies that I believe will help you in your beta reading service immensely.

# PART III

~

"When dealing with people, remember you are not dealing with creatures of logic, but creatures of emotion."

— DALE CARNEGIE

## Did you know?

Dale Carnegie was actually born Dale Carnagey. He was born into poverty on a farm in Missouri. As a student, he participated in the debate team. His excellence in public speaking quickly had other students begging for lessons on how to do the same. He decided not to pursue the family tradition of farming. Once out in the world, he worked as a salesman and found that a great deal of success in life hinges on the power of communication. He became a public speaker and began teaching public speaking courses at YMCAs. Eventually he co-wrote *The Art of Public Speaking* and booked a gig speaking to a sold-out crowd at Carnegie Hall in New York.

I had always assumed that Carnegie Hall was named after him. In fact, it's the reverse. Wanting to be associated with the widely known and revered businessman and philanthropist, Andrew Carnegie, whom the building was actually named after, Dale changed the spelling of his last name from Carnagey to Carnegie.

Interesting, huh?

## FOUR
## THE ACT OF BETA READING
*Let's Do This!*

～

Beta reading is a valuable part of the creative writing and editorial process, as it gives the author the opportunity to receive tips and suggestions on how to tweak, modify, or revise one or more writing elements. This gives them the best chance possible at getting the book close to a finished, publishable work and should include recommendations/referrals for various levels of editing as needed.

We will refer back to the creative writing elements here: theme, setting, time, character, plot, point of view, dialogue, voice, tone, and style. Don't let this overwhelm. It all basically boils down to some simple questions: What happened (plot)? To whom (character)? Where (setting)? When (time)? What did they say (dialogue)? How do you know; as in, who told you (point of view)? How did they say it (voice, tone, and style)? Why did this whole story take place; what's it all mean anyway (theme)?

So how *does* one beta read? I imagine folks have their own methods. I'll share with you what works for me and the authors I've helped. It's really not too complex, I promise. And I know we've covered a lot so far. But once you get started, you'll see it all come together; all the pieces of this puzzle will begin to fall into place. Here is my personal strategy:

**Round 1: The True Read** (Begin filling in the Project

Tracking Worksheet for practice. Link provided in
Chapter 9.)

Read the entire piece (no pencil in hand, no annotation
app fired up, no Track Changes on) harboring the same
anticipation for enjoyment of this book as you would for a
book you've hand-picked from the shelves of your favorite
bookstore. Do not prepare yourself to pick it apart. Just
enjoy the process of reading from beginning to end. This
author has entrusted you with their project that undoubtedly took months to complete. Give them the courtesy of
reading it as a true reader. Be sure to note your start and end
times in the Tracking Worksheet or as a timestamp on the
document itself. (This can simply be a comment out to the
side that says "start 01/01/18 at 8:30 a.m.")

As soon as you finish, write your initial feelings about
this story in your notes. This is not for the author to read,
just something for you to reference. Write in a stream-of-
consciousness manner; just let the words come. No need to
edit. Don't worry about grammar or typos. Just write.

**Address these four areas:**

1. Did you like it? Why or why not? Be thorough.
2. Do you feel it fits the stated genre? Why or why
   not? If you're not sure, think about this during
   your Professional Read (that's round two) and
   mark anything along the way that supports or
   conflicts with the author's stated genre.
   Sometimes, even though they've got the genre
   right, this exercise can help narrow down sub-
   subgenres and keywords they can use for

marketing. (This is one of those underpromise/overdeliver things they'll thank you for.)

3. What do you feel the overall theme was? Can you summarize the story to include the overall theme in one or two sentences? If not, keep this in mind during your Professional Read.

4. Do you feel it has significant editing needs? If so, which ones?

If, during the True Read, you picked up on major story issues or content inconsistencies or typos, you'll need to include this in your letter as a recommendation for professional editing. Be sure to mark them (obviously not all, but a handful should be adequate) during your Professional Read so that you can reference them for support of your recommendation. Answer the questions on the Project Tracking Worksheet.

**Round 2: The Professional Read** (Begin reading over the Professional Read-Through Worksheet. Link provided in Chapter 9.)

In this round you'll read for purposes of notating strengths and weaknesses, asking questions, and making comments for the author's review. You can choose how to flag or keep notes as you read. I'll share my method. Try it. Change it. Do what works for you.

If you've opted to work in Track Changes, you'll have downloaded the document from whatever means the author sent the file to you, saved it to your computer, and opened it in Word. Be sure to enable the Track Changes feature in the Review Tab of the Word ribbon.

If you've opted to work on your iPad, you'll have downloaded the file the author has sent and opened it in the iAnnotate app. Be sure it is saved in a designated folder.

## HERE ARE THE BIG FOUR STEPS OF THE PROFESSIONAL READ:

### STEP ONE:

Fill in as much information as you can in the Tracking Worksheet. At this point, you should be able to complete fields such as the title, pages, chapter pages, time started, etc.

### STEP TWO:

Create your highlighting key in the template. I color coordinate my highlighting with key elements such as POV, characters, setting, etc., as much as possible. I find that sometimes when reading, I may have a question and want to review something I read in earlier chapters but it's not something I'm confident I can find quickly with a word search/navigation. Searching and rereading to look for inconsistencies can take up valuable time. So I highlight key elements as I go. (I usually don't leave this highlighting for the author, FYI; it's just for my personal use. If by chance you do leave it and send it back to the author, just ask them to ignore it; that it's just for your tracking purposes.)

Pick a few elements to start with. You'll most likely add colors as you go.

*Suggested highlighting points:*

**SETTING:** An example would be that I always highlight setting-related text in red. Not entire passages, but just a word or phrase here and there to catch my eye should I need to refer back to it. This comes in very handy for spotting world-building inconsistencies in fantasies as well as ensuring accuracy with historical fiction. Speaking of world-building, I'm a visual learner and therefore find that sketching the world (as I mentioned before) helps me to follow it. Nothing fancy, just make a map, plot some points on it, and reference and build on it as you go. Your author will thank you when you notice that the sisters headed north from city center to the hotel when it was said that the hotel was the *last stop at the south edge of town.*

**TIME LINE:** If a time line is something that is important for the plot, I'll give it a color. For instance, if a character says they climbed Mt. Gargantuan in four days, and then a telling of that climb revealed that the crew had set out to climb that mountain, camping and sleeping along the way, you can highlight each sleep scene or wake scene (or any clue to a new day) in blue to help track the days (if the days are laid out as such.) If the story keeps plugging along and you feel like they should be there already, you can quickly scan for blue blocks. If you find you've highlighted six days of this four-day trek, you can leave a comment for the author and easily refer them to each instance.

**CHARACTER:** I give each important character a color, especially when it comes to descriptions. That way if I'm all the way to Chapter 9 and read something about Charlie's *sea green eyes* but am pretty sure I remember them being *black as night* in earlier chapters, I can quickly scan the previous pages for his assigned highlighter color. This can pay off in many ways. Once you get to reading, you'll feel the need (even if you're not sure why yet) to mark areas here and there—just in case you may want to reference it later. I say go for it. It's for your eyes only anyways. And having it color coordinated makes returning to a character so much easier, as the author is not going to preface each description with the character's name, making using the navigation/search tool futile.

Another character example is, say, in Chapter 2 the narrator mentions that *Harris hated being an only child— every sense of the phrase "only child" stabbed at his heart, especially since he'd once had a brother, but that brother and Harris's mom both died in a house fire.* And then later Harris mentions that his *mother drank too much, stayed numb, ever since the house fire.* Something to note to the author if this isn't cleared up somewhere in the story. I mean, how's she gonna drink too much; she's dead, right?

For the author, having a completed character sketch which includes an arc can help avoid these issues. If when reading, you find this to be an area of weakness that rears its head frequently, I would recommend offering the author a character sketch form. Not all authors have heard of such a thing and would be grateful to receive one. Writing 300-plus pages and keeping up with character details can be a challenge, even if you are the one who has created those details to begin with.

Also, as a beta reader, if you can't point out how a character evolved throughout the story, their arc, you should mention this to the author. Detail inconsistencies and meager character arcs can be remedied with the use of a character sketch. A character sketch can be a total game changer for an author (and any others providing input on the work).

**POV**: You can also highlight for POV and tense if you start feeling like maybe it's hopping around. Sometimes this problem area sneaks in and you're not sure when or where exactly the change happened. For instance, the story starts off being told in the first-person POV by the main character and in the present tense. This is used for suspense a lot. So it will read something like this:

*I try to be as quiet as I can, breathe slowly. But my heart is pounding, making my breaths loud and choppy. I know he can hear me. I see his snakeskin boots step right up to the edge of the bed. I look around. There's nowhere I can go. I brace myself, prepare myself. If he bends down and looks under this bed, my only defense is to jab my fingers into his eyes.*

Then a few chapters later it reads like this:

*Jenny ran straight into the sliding glass door, nose first. Stunned, she felt the panic drift away along with all sound and color. When she woke, she felt a throbbing pain in her head and saw the blurred snakeskin boots slowly come into clarity.*

Here you can see that the narration switched from being told **by** Jenny in the **present tense** (in the now) to being told **about** Jenny in the **past tense** (a recounting). This is a frequent slip among many early writers; so I make a point to highlight POV and tense from the very beginning and check it as the story unfolds.

By the way, it's not unheard of for the POV to change, or even the tense, but it needs to be intentional and done in a way that's not distracting or jolting (and takes a great deal of writing skill to pull off).

**THEME:** Many times, an author will write with a theme in mind. Or sometimes, they just form organically as they write. Either way, a reader should be able to pick up on it. (You can see what their intended theme was by referring back to the author questionnaire.)

When you come across passages and events that support a theme, highlight them. By identifying these areas, you can return to them afterwards and see how well they maintained consistency. You may even spot more than one. And that's fine as long as each is clear. If the theme seems solid and clear, you'll be able to refer back to this to share with the author what you, as the reader, felt the theme was. Hopefully what you took away from the story aligns with their intentions. If the theme seems inconsistent or fizzles out or is unidentifiable, you can at least refer to passages and events and consistent tone within word choices that they can consider using to build upon.

Remember, the story has to have an underlying purpose for having been written. Identifying elements of theme for the author provides a great opportunity for them to revise these themes (if necessary) so they can make them more engaging throughout the story.

Theme is probably the hardest of these elements to grasp for both writers and readers and can take some time and study to nail down. If you'd like to see what themes are out there in published works, try Googling a book title and the word "theme." Oftentimes, if the book is fairly established, you'll find online studies or notes that will include themes. This is a helpful way to get a feel for how themes are articulated. As an example, search "Hunger Games theme" and see what you come up with.

**STEP THREE:**

You should have already familiarized yourself with the Professional Read-Through Worksheet to get your mind geared up and focused. If not, hop to it.

As you read the work (the book you've selected), read with intention. Read to identify. Notice where your attention hits snags, where your focus fails. Did you have to read something more than once for it to make sense? If so, highlight and make a note saying so. Did you finish reading a section or scene and wonder why it was there, what purpose it served? Note that.

Equally as important, note areas of strength and passages that stand out as really great and say why. It's easy to point out the areas that need work. But when it comes to crafting your feedback, you'll need to reflect on strengths just as often as weaknesses, as authors need to know what is working just as much as what is not. So be sure to mark them and comment why they are strong. (And if you stay on top of this while you read, you won't be struggling to remember the good stuff when it comes time to craft your analysis/letter.)

Be sure to write your notes in a way that makes sense to you. You can polish them up later. The point is to alert the author of any areas that slow the reader and detract from the story, as well as bolster the writing and work as a whole.

Be generous with your markups, highlighting, questions, and comments as you read, and fill in the Tracking Worksheet and Professional Read-Through Worksheet along the way. Keeping substantial notes during this process will make authoring your analysis/letter that much easier. Scant notes may land you in the crickets zone when it comes time to craft your feedback. Remember, during this process, the marking up is for your eyes only—you'll clean it all up before submitting to your author—so don't worry about perfection. And obviously, the more beta reading you do, the more efficient and skilled you'll become at writing these notes and comments. Just like with any other skill set.

**STEP FOUR:**

Keep your eyes peeled for areas to support recommendations for professional editing. Any large-scale issues, especially when there are many, will likely need a developmental edit. So if you feel addressing these issues may take more than the author can handle, say it.

Consistent problems with sentence structure that lead to choppy, confusing, or convoluted lines could be remedied with a line editor.

Contextual flaws, grammar mistakes, and clear lack of understanding of punctuation may warrant a copyeditor.

And for the love of all things literary, always recommend the work to be proofed by a professional proofreader before it is published.

In the case where you feel the writer is just too far off the mark, you can also recommend helpful articles and books, author sites, classes, or even hiring a writing coach.

Be sure to highlight enough of these areas so that you can refer back to them to support your recommendation.


That's the gist of the two read-throughs. But I know you want more concrete suggestions of things that might slow a reader or require consideration. The following is a list of questions and aspects to consider during the Professional Read. They are included in the Professional Read-Through Worksheet, but I'll discuss a few of them in more detail here. It's not an exhaustive list, and each and every one need not be considered, but it certainly will help you as a beta reader when you have trouble pinpointing why something feels off. Hope it helps!


**Did you get hooked early on?**

In other words, did the story generate enough interest early on to make you want to read more? Or did you have to "get through" pages or even chapters before you felt something interesting started happening?

Sometimes, it's not that the writing isn't interesting; it's that the author may have started the story in the wrong place, expecting patience from the reader as they meticulously set the stage. In this ain't-nobody-got-time-fa-dat day and age, trying to set the stage can be a huge risk. If a reader doesn't feel hooked in the first few pages, they'll likely close the book. Think about the "Look Inside" feature Amazon provides its readers. It's akin to a person standing in a bookstore, picking up a book, and reading through the first few pages. They're not going to stand there and read two chapters to decide whether or not to commit, to buy. The same happens with the "Look Inside" feature—but with more limitations. Depending upon what percentage the author allows in the "Look Inside," the reader may not even have the option to continue reading, as the preview can be short. So then what? The reader didn't get hooked; the preview is done. Eh. Next. No sale.

If this seems to be a potential issue for the story you're beta reading, consider how this could be remedied. I often try to identify a few provocative or interesting lines as close to the beginning as possible and then consider how the story might change if it began there. It's always best to suggest something as a remedy if you're going to knock a writer's opening. This is my go-to remedy: find something they already have that sparks interest and build from there.

If you feel the scene setting is necessary but doesn't hook the reader, you can suggest the writer open with a grabbing scene and then immediately come back to the scene-setting element. There are always options. Sometimes it just takes a few tries to get it right. As a beta reader, it's not your place to "fix" this for the author, but I find offering up a potential solution or two helps the author to think outside their current work.

## Are the characters fully developed?

Do they feel real? Are they unique? Does each have a purpose?

Character development can range depending upon the character's role. Obviously, the main character will need to be fully developed with identifiable and distinct qualities: goals and motivations, voice, challenges, flaws, history. Secondary characters need not be as fully developed, but it should be enough so that their presence enhances the story. If you can't make out what a character's purpose is, try imagining the story without them. Maybe they need to be cut. Maybe they need more work. Be sure to share these considerations with your author.

Once you've identified the characteristics of each cast member, you can keep your eyes peeled for inconsistencies or missing elements that leave the character flat or contrived.

If, when reading, you find yourself asking *Why did he do this* or saying *I don't feel like he would do this*, it may reveal that the character's motivations aren't clear.

Oftentimes, if I find I can't make much distinction between characters, meaning they have no unique voices, mannerisms, names, etc., I'll suggest the author create character sketches. A character sketch is basically a Q & A about a specific character that fleshes out even the smallest of details, such as a nervous tick, signature phrase, or childhood fear. If an author has set about writing without fully exploring and creating characters, they can all kind of blur together—even blur with the narration. And then the reader is forced to struggle to keep everyone sorted out. Character sketches can draw out unique details to include so that each character becomes easily recognizable, just by their habits, word choices, subtle actions, etc.

If you read and find you can't remember who does what, can't remember who is whom, keep mixing people up, it may be that the characters just aren't developed enough. It could also be that their names are too similar. Having a Kristin, Kristy, and Kaitlyn all in one story can get confusing. Just something to keep in mind.

It's also helpful to keep track of which characters you like and which you don't. Then consider why. Not all characters are meant to be liked. But it helps the author to know why a reader feels a certain way about their characters. More than anything, there needs to be characters that are relatable. If a reader can't find any connection with a character, can't empathize, can't root for them to succeed or fail, they'll have no emotional investment in the story. This is true even of antagonists.

It's just as important that the antagonist, even if you want them to fail, be fully developed and have some sort of relatable quality. Maybe her "flaw" is a weakness for the underdog. Maybe his relatable feature is a constant hankering for candy. In life, we aren't typically in disagreement with every single aspect of a person that we dislike. This should be true even of the villain. Most people aren't born evil. So a great way to develop a villain is to give them some humanity; show just how they came to be so terrible. And not all antagonists are evil. They may simply stand in the way of the protagonist's success. To round out the antagonist, make it known what their goals are and why. There are usually some relatable gems hidden here.

So if you read and find you have no connections whatsoever with any member of the cast, explore why and share that information with your author. Equally as important, point out the characters you love and say why. It can help the writer identify where they've nailed their character development at times so that they can carry it over to other characters in the story.

## How was the pacing of the plot?

Did you find areas that were absolutely page-turning good? Were some sections boring? Was anything confusing? Did you ever want to quit on the book? Identify these areas and explore why you feel the way you do. Regarding pacing, if the story is blasting along, then you find a few chapters that drag, let the author know this. Maybe they can insert some action or a mini-conflict. Maybe they can rearrange some scenes. Maybe they need to cut some things.

If a section or two was so great you couldn't wait to read more, say this. If you can, say why. Maybe it's because the author did a great job at building suspense. Maybe it's because a character was so well developed that you got attached. Maybe the imagery and emotional draw in a love scene was spot on. Whatever the reason, share this positive experience with the author.

If you got bored in areas, mark them and consider why. Do you feel the writing here contributes to the story? Maybe it's not necessary. If you think it does need to stay, what can the author do to liven it up? Maybe the writing fell into a narrative information dump and can be converted into action and dialogue scenes to deliver the same message.

If you got confused anywhere, it's very important to mark it and let the author know this. It's so easy, as a writer, to keep important information locked inside your mind, thinking you've adequately written everything a reader might need. Or maybe the confusion lies in the sentence construction. Oftentimes, a sentence can be reworded to bring about greater clarity. If you find this to be the case many times throughout the manuscript, a recommendation for line editing may be warranted.

And if you ever just wanted to quit on a book, think long and hard about why. I first make every attempt to look within myself before considering telling an author I had trouble sticking with their book. Consider these things: you aren't reading a genre you prefer (this is why it's so important to read only in genres you enjoy—you see how it could potentially result in unwarranted negative feedback?); the story itself touches a nerve, drags up some emotion you prefer not to experience or memory you prefer to keep suppressed; a character reminds you of someone you don't wish to spend time with or reminds you of aspects of yourself you don't like or aren't proud of; you are in deep disagreement with the theme and feel completely at odds with the intended message (political, moral, religious conflicts). There's nothing wrong with feeling any of these ways. What's important here is to consider whether or not you can give this author a fair read. If you can't, it is important to say so and come to an agreement with the author whether to continue or not.

If you don't find anything personal at the heart of your struggle to read this book, then you need to identify what it is about the writing or story that makes you want to quit. Writing is no easy feat and is not for everyone. Just as singing is not for everyone. But I fully believe it's everyone's right to pursue the things they love. I'm not ever going to tell an author that they're basically barking up the wrong tree, setting themselves up for failure, or doomed. What I will do is make sure that I'm honest about their weaknesses and direct them to someone or something that can help them grow their skills.

So please never think that because you don't like something that you ever have the right to tell someone to quit. Instead, consider this a personal challenge to help out someone with passion. So find the weaknesses—maybe it's that they have unbelievably poor grammar that's crazy distracting; maybe the story just doesn't make sense at all; maybe their writing style is a turn-off (too flowery, too fanciful); maybe the story is filled with pages of clichés—whatever the reason, point it out and make a suggestion that would help you, as a reader, enjoy the story more.

**Was the story arc easy to follow?**

Were there any holes in the story? Was it plausible (given the genre and context overall)? Was the ending satisfying?

As you are reading and come across confusion in the story arc, sometimes in the form of missing elements or plot holes, comment with a question. If you're uncertain as to how the characters ended up where they did, maybe the author forgot to write in some important scene transitions. Or maybe you can't figure out what happened to a character; they just fell off the pages. Bring this up. Your questions in the comment bubbles can help them to go back and logically revise.

The same can be said in regard to plausibility. "Believable" is a relative term when it comes to fiction. Obviously, fantasy isn't believable in the sense that a family drama is. That's not what I'm talking about. What you want to note is when something that happens in the story isn't believable within the story's context. Maybe it's not believable, given a character's history, that she would participate in the killing of the antagonist. Maybe the progression of an illness isn't believable and the author should research more. Be sure to note these reservations you may have about plausibility and say why.

The same is true with the ending. Readers who have just invested hours, days, sometimes weeks of their lives want to be rewarded with a satisfying ending. That doesn't mean a happy ending per se, but an ending that has a resolution that is plausible given the last 300 or so pages they've just read. This is where conventions sometimes come into play. Be sure to review for any ending-specific genre conventions when considering your analysis of the final pages.

**Is the tone consistent throughout the work?**

Is the language and word choice a contributing or distracting factor? Is the dialogue purposeful?

The story should have a consistent tone. And this can be achieved with proper word choice and sentence structure. Consider how differently these two lines read:

Affectionate tone: *I watched as the tiny pup nestled its way into the pile of linens.*

Repulsed tone: *I cringed as the mangy mutt clawed away at the dirty laundry.*

If the story's tone, voice, and style are meant to be a certain way, make sure the words and sentences make it so.

When considering the contributing or distracting nature of words, I hone in on the writer's use, lack, or abuse of passive verbs and descriptive words such as adverbs and adjectives. A weak word choice is often the use of a passive "to be" verb paired with an overly descriptive word or two. Also common is when the writer overwrites in an effort to seem...writerly. This comes about with the overuse of fanciful words. It's like they ran their manuscript through some sort of auto-thesaurus. Here are a few examples of when word choice, weak words, and poor syntax become distracting:

*The soiled, dirty laundry arranged in a pile upon the floor was endlessly clawed at by the stinky, dirty, mangy mutt. I was disgusted as my nose perceived the stench. It made me recoil compulsorily. I begrudgingly remarked, "Um, so yeah. Does he have to stay here?"*

These lines are weak in that there's the passive verb choice, an overuse of adjectives and adverbs, and a wordy sentence structure that's difficult to follow. If I restructure the sentence, replace the verbs, and cut out some of the fanciful words—basically just cut to the chase—the reader won't have to translate all this.

*The mangy mutt clawed the dirty laundry piled in the floor. I recoiled at its stench. I said, "Does he have to stay here?"*

Sometimes, clarity beats fanciful. And I'm not saying the above example is the best and only way to rework these lines. But if you find the author's attempts at creating memorable prose becomes more distracting than useful, note it. If it occurs throughout the manuscript, highlight a few areas to reference. If you can, try a rework of one or two to see if it brings clarity while keeping the author's voice. Then make a general statement about it in your letter, maybe recommending a line editor if it's significant.

.  .  .

Dialogue can easily make or break a story. In an effort to make dialogue seem realistic, authors will sometimes write as they might hear it out in the real world. This can result in wordy and useless dialogue—no different than many conversations we endure in reality, right? No need to force a reader into the same mundane silence-filling talks. If you can't make out the purpose for a piece of dialogue, it may need to be cut or reworked. If it doesn't reveal something about a character, an event, a motivation, the setting, some foreshadowing, then question it. And oftentimes, dialogue needs to be trimmed. Consider a real conversation:

*I said, "Hey, Mom."*
*Mom said: "Hey, hon."*
*I asked, "What's that?"*
*Mom said, "What's what?"*
*I asked, "That thing in your hand?"*
*Mom asked, "Oh, this?"*
*I said, "Yeah."*
*Mom said, "Your locket."*

....unless whatever is in her hand is some sort of weapon, something to reveal useful information, this whole mess should be cut.

And even if there is something useful in her hand, the dialogue still could use some trimming.

*I asked, "Mom, what's that in your hand?"*
*Mom said, "Hon, they found your locket."*

And these lines were here to reveal that Mom finding the locket means she knows her daughter was at the scene of the crime or whatever. The point is, even though we may naturally speak with all this extra business, it serves no purpose in writing. Be sure to identify for the author any areas that "suffer" from this useless dialogue. And if the story is riddled with it, note a few places and include the general observation in your letter.

## Do you feel immersed in the story, its characters, setting, actions, etc.?

Do you get a well-rounded sense of everything described? Sometimes, it can be that we've only been told a story and the author has failed to let us see it, smell it, taste it, and feel it. Sensory details can really bring a story to life.

It's common to say that Jane had blond hair and freckles. It might be easier, though, to get a real sense of her if we also know that, each time she passes by, Mark breathes in the sweet mango shampoo of her hair. It's common to say the diner had black and white tile with red tables and a juke box in the corner. But maybe you'd really feel you were in that diner if you heard the juke box and the crashing dishes, smelled the mixture of bitter coffee and grease, noticed how each overhead lamp hung above the tables like a spotlight. Including elements of sound, taste, smell, light, tactile sensations, visceral responses, etc., can really help a reader to become fully immersed in a story. Keep this in mind if you find you're struggling to do so. (By the way, in the writerly world, this is known as "show; don't tell".)

Beta reading incorporates both macro and micro feedback. The macro feedback covers any overarching strengths, weaknesses, or questions that may impact the overall novel and is addressed in the letter/analysis. Micro feedback covers minor points that can be identified and addressed within the inline comments and can also be covered in the letter if you find they occur in abundance. If you've made use of your highlighting tools, note and comments features, the Tracking Worksheet, as well as the Professional Read-

Through Worksheet, you should have plenty of material to use in crafting your feedback.

I'm sure you feel at this point you'd like to just send what you have and let the author read it over. Please refrain. Quick comments and questions and highlights can be interpreted as negative, unclear, dismissive, sometimes even snarky. If you want to truly help your author, you've got to compile your information in an easy-to-follow, concise, and constructive manner. That's where the letter and analysis come in.

## COMPILING YOUR DATA

Because you've taken such excellent inline notes, compiling them will be a breeze.

**MICROSOFT WORD:** In Word, you can either scroll from page 1 to what feels like infinity trying to make sense of your notes, or you can export them into one nice and neat report. Here's how:

- Open the document. The comments should show up immediately. If they don't, click on the **Review** tab in your Word ribbon. Select **All Markup.**
- Under **Show Markup**, which is situated just below, select **Specific People**>[**your name**] (or however you're identified in your computer).

*fig 11*

- Now click on the **File** tab.
- Select **Print.** At this point, you can either actually print the pages (which seems unnecessary to me) or create a PDF document and save it (no wasted paper, right?).
- To create a PDF, select **Microsoft Print to PDF** in the printer dropdown menu.

*fig 12*

- Under **Settings** click on **Print All Pages dropdown** and select **List of Markup.** Note that once you do this, your print preview won't update. But when you create it, it will produce a list of annotations instead of the document.

*fig 13*

- Now click **Print**. This will open a window where you can choose where to save the PDF. I would save it in the file you've created for your author. When you open the document, it will look something like this. (Be sure to read the comments in the figure below; they are part of this instruction.)

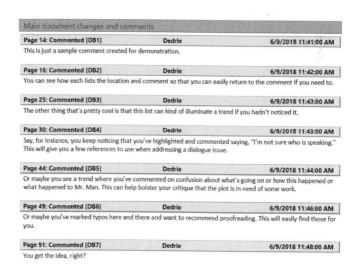

*fig 14*

You have the document saved and can print it if you so choose. So now you've got all your comments readily available. Yay!

**IANNOTATE:** If you're doing this with iAnnotate, here's how you'll accomplish the same thing:

- To create a PDF of all the annotations, tap the **Email PDF Summary** tool in the toolbar (as shown below).

*fig 15*

- It will bring up an email window with the PDF already attached.
- Rather than emailing the document, you can tap on it to open, then tap the share icon in the top right corner to send it to iAnnotate, or Add to Notes, or you can copy it to your Google Drive. Wherever works for you is fine. I usually just send it to iAnnotate so that I can flip back and forth between the manuscript, my letter and analysis, and my compiled comments.
- Another option is to create a note in your tablet

by selecting the **Email Annotation Summary** tool (looks like this):

*fig 16*

It will also open an email. Touch and hold somewhere in the body of the email (all your annotations) until an options bar pops up. Tap **Select All**, then tap **Copy**.

- Now go to your Notes app in your tablet. Open a new note and paste the contents. Title it for your author's work and save the note.

There are more than a few ways to accomplish these tasks in both Word and iAnnotate. I'm just getting you going. You may soon find a way that better suits you.

The act of beta reading will certainly take up the bulk of your time and requires some skill and knowledge that can be taught. But transforming that information into actionable feedback an author will be receptive to takes tact and the creativity to turn what may seem like criticism into welcomed help. This, my friend, takes great thought and practice.

Anyone can send their quick notes and knee-jerk opinions. It's the successful beta reader that can craft those impressions into something that bolsters the author's desire to continue their work. I don't know that I can teach tact— I've come to learn that not everybody possesses such an important quality in life—but I'll certainly give it a try.

# FIVE

# THE ART OF CRAFTING FEEDBACK
*What Winston Churchill and Southerners Have in Common*

Beta feedback can play an integral role in the publishing journey. In fact, the feedback you give the author in your analysis could influence every step the author takes afterward; therefore, crafting articulate, helpful, and actionable feedback is nothing to take lightly. I know some people think beta reading isn't such a big deal, that it's just opinions (everybody's got one). But I take my role as a beta reader very seriously. For an author, letting another person read your work can be an exceptionally trying, vulnerable, and scary thing, especially since much of creative writing draws from personal thoughts, feelings, emotions, and experiences. And the last thing a beta reader needs to do is lose sight of that.

So let's talk about the art of crafting feedback. I call it an art because it takes some thoughtful consideration and word wizardry on top of learned skills. It's easy to tell someone that you loved their main character because they've done such a thorough job of development. It's not so easy to come up with helpful words when you feel the plot makes no sense, or that their writing is damn near incomprehensible due to the mass of fanciful adverbs, or that the story was so boring it made you want to ask them if they nodded off a few times while writing the dreaded thing. These are the times when you've got to get creative, in part because you need to find the most charming and tactful way to relay this information, in part because you need to be able to offer up some sort of help so that they don't just shut the whole thing down and crawl into a deep, dark hole.

To tackle these things, I draw from two sources: Winston Churchill's quote on tact and my Southern roots. Winston Churchill once said, "Tact is the ability to tell someone to go to hell in such a way that they look forward to the trip." Obviously, this is a bit extreme, but you get the idea. It's about message delivery and keeping the receiver open to these things you need them to hear. I know that if someone is spewing some rude and thoughtless criticism my way, I'll shut it down real fast (and risk missing some really valuable information hidden within the tactless attempt).

An excellent example would be my conversation with the first editor I reached out to when writing this series. This person clearly had a moment of failed tact. I'm giving her the benefit of the doubt when I say a moment—this could have just been her way. I do not know. But in that "moment," she actually read aloud one of my lines to me and then said, quote/unquote, I hate this. I didn't hire her. Not because she didn't like something I had written, but because she lacked the ability to express that in a graceful and professional way. I'm not gonna pay someone to be an ass to me when I can get the same service but with someone who knows that support and encouragement are vital, as well as possesses some basic manners.

I'll be honest, I partly blamed this on her New York-ed-ness. (I think I just made up a word.) New Yorkers have been known to shoot straight from the hip. But that's a terrible stereotype, right? I'm sure not all do. I mean, I certainly don't want to be typed as a hillbilly bimbo blond. But I do like to think that Southerners are known, in part at least, for their hospitality and manners.

Manners, by the way, is swiftly becoming a thing of the

past. Somehow, folks got the idea that freedom to be yourself and say what you want equates to setting all manners and respect for others aside, that our personal thoughts and ideas and ideals are to be known and heard at any cost. I totally disagree with this. I think every word that leaves a person's mouth should be preceded by a thought or two about how it could harm another. Even more so, these words need great consideration when the method of delivery is the written word. It's easy to thoughtlessly type the thing you wish you could say, far easier than speaking it. But always try to place yourself on the receiving end of those words. Imagine that you are the one who just spent four years writing this thing you're so proud of and then reading some quipped sarcastic remark like "What does this even mean???" If you can do that, really summon up some empathy, I think you'll make better choices when it comes to expressing your opinions.

In all honesty, even though I didn't hire that editor, and even though I thought she could use a lesson or two in manners, I did find some of her approach useful. I don't have a thin skin. I don't really care a whole lot about if everyone loves my work. I do hope it can be of use to at least one person. And it would be dang super if it helped a whole lot of folks. But I don't need the approval of others. Because of this, I was able to consider all the other things this editor had to say. She posed some pretty forward objections, which ultimately, probably to her dismay, grounded me even stronger in my desire to write this series. Her fear was that betas might step on the toes of editors, take their jobs. This couldn't be further from the truth, as I always stress the value in pointing out editorial needs when teaching the art of beta reading. What I mean to say is, her straightforward opinions served a purpose. They were clear. And from them,

I was able to get more grounded in my mission. So the take-away is to shoot straight, but do so with tact and the desire to be gracious and helpful. Like I said at the get-go, sugar-coating does nothing to improve the writing and tactless remarks make for an inhospitable working relationship. And inhospitable relationships will mean no future work for you.

*Okay, I get it, Dedrie! I promise not to be a jerk. But how do I craft the feedback?*

## THE LETTER

Okay, so you now have all your notes in a list form. It's time to think about the letter. I fully believe in the double-decker sandwich approach when it comes to feedback and crafting a letter. So each piece of bread serves as the praise; the fixin's (or your meat, veggies, and cheese) serve as the constructive criticism. So ya got a slice of bread on top, then some fixin's, another piece of bread, more fixin's, and finally the bottom piece of bread which is thick enough to hold up this towering sammich. That means starting off with an overall positive remark, getting into some areas to consider, pointing out some things that are working well, getting into the nitty-gritty, and then finally getting to the greatest of their strengths. Sprinkled and drizzled all throughout this sandwich are some seasonings and special sauce; that's the intended helpful suggestions and recommendations.

Now before you go thinking that including positive remarks and strengths only serve to butter them up for your criticisms, think again. If someone is not told what they do well, they won't know to keep doing it. If someone isn't told where their strengths lie, they may not tap into them. If someone isn't told what a great scene they've written, they may cut it. So positive feedback is just as essential as the negative.

I always like to kick off my letter with a very positive first paragraph. This includes opening with my appreciation for their willingness to share their work with me and how I always feel honored to be a part of this creative process. Then I'll offer my best summary of the book (in one to two lines) and how I felt their writing reflects something they seem passionate about, whether it's their love of beautiful language or writing in general or the subject of the novel—and how I or other readers have or will relate to that. Maybe it's a story about the underdog coming out on top and you feel many people will relate; maybe it's a thriller about a mass murderer and their attention to detail was perfect for conveying that intended thrill; maybe it's a love story between two teenage girls and you feel this subject is greatly needed in the YA genre; maybe it's an adventure about dogs and you just love anything and everything about dogs and can easily see that they do too. You need to find something that reflects that writer's interest and/or passion and comment that their love for this thing shines through in their writing.

Next mention something you particularly enjoyed about the book and why. Again, this could be their style, the story, a character, the ending, anything. If it's their first book and you feel it went overall pretty well, be sure to give this praise for a debut author. If it's their tenth book and you feel they've done a good job, you can mention how their writing seems seasoned. If by chance you are struggling to find anything positive to say here, mention that you're eager to share your feedback on their hard work. The point of this paragraph is to 1) create a sense of enthusiasm on your part for working on their book, 2) let it be known that you get the gist of the work, 3) make them aware that you're equally interested in their strengths, not just weaknesses, and 4) hopefully knock off a little intimidation or anxiety they may be experiencing while reading/anticipating your feedback.

The next paragraph will start to fade into the constructive criticisms. But I still like the first sentence to be positive and to strive for a sense of ease on the author's end. I like to begin this paragraph by sharing my process with them. This establishes some value for your work. So many times, we work hard on something and then present one or two pages, and it can be easy to falsely think that it didn't take all that much effort. So I begin by reminding them that this is not an edit, but that I am passionate about this work and do my best to offer any and every bit of helpful feedback that I can; that yes, these are just my opinions, the opinions of a well-read [Mystery/YA/whatever] genre lover and skilled beta reader. I then tell them that I read their manuscript in its entirety twice: once in the leisurely way I would read for pleasure and then once with intention. If I sketched a map, I'll be sure to mention this so they know I've tracked their world-building for accuracy. If I personally have knowledge about something they've written, I'll mention that. If you were once a lawyer and this is a crime novel, you can mention your expertise and that you enjoyed being able to apply that knowledge to the beta reading process of their manuscript. If you grew up in a certain area and have intimate knowledge of the story's setting, you can share that. These are just further attempts to give the author some faith in your upcoming words.

Now you can start to tackle specific areas. You are not going to tear this person apart by mentioning every single flaw. I find that if you structure the feedback in sections, this keeps it focused and concise and allows you to touch on things that will flip back and forth between strengths and weaknesses.

Use the worksheet and the topics discussed in the previous chapter to guide you. You can even use headings and group topics if you prefer. I'll not go over again all the things that you could address since you've been provided tons of elements to consider, but I will give a few examples of how to word the feedback so that it is better received and something the author can work with.

Say you've got a novel that takes a considerable amount of time to get to the hook. (Remember, the sooner the better with the hook. Line 1 would be the best-case scenario. Somewhere on page 1, the next best. If the book has lost the reader before the story ever starts, there's no point to any other feedback, so be thorough here. Also, it's not a set-in-stone rule that the hook must fall on page 1, so use your judgment.) There's a lot of background, setting the scene, a rather slow and uneventful build. It's basically two chapters of "are we there yet" kind of stuff. Locate the first possible point of intrigue in the writing or a good impactful line and suggest it as a starting point. You could say something like this:

*That early scene with Donovan and his mom where she finds the gun is really strong. Would you consider making this the attention-grabbing opener for this work? As you know, readers require an interesting hook, something to make them want to read more, and they need it as soon as possible (first line or first page is ideal...since unfortunately the human race has whittled its attention span down to that of a goldfish).*

*Your hook occurs a bit too late in the book, not until 41 pages in. I get that you are giving some background for the reader, kind of setting up the story. But my fear is that you may lose many readers by this point. That scene on page 41 where Donovan and his mom are in a heated conversation could be a great starting point.*

*What if you started the book there, and then once you hooked the reader, you could swing back around to some of the background you've got in the previous pages?*

Do you see how I used a strength to address a weakness? Rather than saying *your first two chapters dragged* or *you took too long to get anywhere* or *I didn't like the first part of the story*, find a way to use what good they've done to address the "bad." Also, if at all possible, I try to toss in any bit of (appropriate) humor to keep things light, i.e., the goldfish remark. If humor is not your thing, ignore this. But if you find that you set people at ease with some light humor, then use it to your advantage. It will only help the author relax.

Maybe this author has gone a little adverb crazy or used an exorbitant amount of fanciful words that all seem to clutter up the message. Sometimes it can get frustrating to read these lines. You find yourself having to translate. It can be very easy to scold the writer to the tune of *your writing is so over the top that I can barely follow what you're trying to say.* Instead, try something like this:

*It is clear that you place great effort in your writing and you've gone to great lengths to capitalize on literary elements such as metaphor and simile. I admire that. Regarding some of these, however, might I suggest considering their efficacy. I think your writing strength allows for stronger and more active verb choices that wouldn't require such fanciful and detracting adverbs and adjectives. There were areas that I found slowed my reading, areas that I believe you could easily strengthen with more concise language. Sometimes, simple works better. I've marked a few passages for your review in this area as well as some passages where you've really done a fantastic job so that you may compare them.*

Again, even though I'm doling out some criticism here in the writing style, I'm pulling in areas where the author wrote some very good lines. You could even cite one or two strong lines against one or two weak ones to point out the difference. Just be sure the author can see where she has written a great line that supports your point.

If there's a developmental issue with a character, you can say something to the effect of this:

*As a reader, I had a difficult time believing that Donovan would have killed himself over what Berkley did. It seemed rash given what we know about Donovan. This leads me to believe that maybe I'm not totally clear on Donovan's motivations and fears and mental instability. So I would recommend further character development of Donovan.*

*Maybe you could show us his emotional instability more in some previous scenes. A really great scene is when he catches his mother with his best friend. Maybe you can draw out more of his reactions here, show us how unstable he can be when faced with difficult situations.*

Here, you can see that I've pointed out a pretty big flaw, the underdevelopment of the author's main character (identifying weakness), and then pointed out a strong scene (positive) that she could incorporate to show us more about Donovan as a person (suggestion).

Once you've identified some areas that need attention, typically some big ones (I like to get them out of the way first), I then move to pointing out some strengths. These are easy to word but sometimes hard to find unless you've made a conscious effort to highlight them along the way. As humans, we are drawn to point out flaws so easily, aren't we? Be sure to list a few significant strengths or parts you really enjoyed and why. The *why* is so important; otherwise, it's just flattery. And flattery doesn't make for stronger work.

*Your ability to build tension throughout this story is exemplary. The slow build was expertly paced, and by the time Jackson and Dave met in the marina, I was sitting on the edge of my seat!*

*Your use of imagery, especially when describing the setting, is effective. In fact, I would say it's your strongest writing quality. I could easily place myself in the boat, smell the ocean, feel the queasiness and fear that Jackson felt. And when he and his son are tossed overboard, I felt his anxiety as he scrambled to find his son in the thrashing waters. Really great job!*

So we've tackled the top bread (positive), the first layer of fixin's (critique), the middle bread (more positive), and now we need a layer of critique and a final hefty layer of positive to support the whole lot and wrap up the letter. I like this next layer of critique to be the place where I ask any big questions I may have as well as point out any needs for professional editing services. Questions require a little less finesse than pointing out weaknesses, but still be mindful of your tone and be sure to explain why you have the question. Like any other area, tag on a positive.

*I didn't feel there were any major plot holes, but I did have a few questions after finishing. James's character seemed integral to the subplot when the story takes place in New York, and I thought you did a great job of developing him to the level that you did. I realize he's not one of the main characters, but it seemed he kind of just disappeared. I was left wondering, what happened to James? Do you feel you completed James's story arc?*

*And then also, I was a bit confused about Mary's aunt and the restaurant scene. It wasn't clear to me when this all was occurring. Was this a flashback? Is this scene important? If so, I would suggest elaborating more and maybe working in a scene transition like you did for the subway flashback scene. If you don't think it really propels the story, maybe consider cutting it.*

*And my biggest question, what motivated Charlie to leave? Should I know this? I feel like I missed something. If you can't point to areas that lead up to this, maybe revisit Charlie's character and develop his character arc a bit more. All the other character stories were well-written and strong. I just felt I missed a little bit with Charlie.*

So again, you can see that each question gives a reason for the question, something positive, and a suggestion. One thing to note about asking questions—try to avoid the *why* question. *Why* questions tend to put the receiver on the defense. So instead of saying *Why did you do this thing*, you can use some of these prompts:

- How did [James find out about the gun]? I wasn't able to determine this from the reading.
- I don't understand [Mary's motivation when it comes to her leaving].
- [Benjamin] comes across as [angry]. Is that how you see him?
- The detail of [whatever it is] seems [to slow the pace]. Is there a way to give it more relevance? If not, is it necessary to the whole of the story?
- In the final scene, did you want to express a tone of [sadness]? I wasn't certain if it was sadness or irritation that I would feel if I was in Jeremy's shoes.
- Mr. Jameson's goal seems to be [this]. Do I have that right? I'm not solid on this.
- I was confused during the scene where [Marissa walks into the bank and then runs out]. What was her motivation in that scene?

You get the idea, right? Don't ask *why* the author chose

to write something. Be more concise in your questions, and the author will have greater ease at addressing them.

Regarding the recommendation of professional editing services, always mention that you are aware that the author is still in the revision process (unless you happen to know otherwise), and that it may be some time before she is ready to move to the next phase, but that you feel it's important to mention. If there are significant and obvious overall writing limitations, I might recommend some resources for creative writing or a writing coach. Some developmental editors offer this service to those who struggle overall with the process. It's not an easy thing to tell someone that their work is nowhere near where it needs to be and that you doubt it will get there without professional help. But this is the kindest thing you can do for someone who wants to be a published (and well-received) author. Do not shy away here. This ultimately could be your most important contribution toward this person's dream. Here are some examples:

*It's always an honor to work with writers, and I take my role very seriously. Part of that role, I feel, is to ensure the writer knows all the wonderful services available to them, services that can help them produce the best work possible. After the two read-throughs of [A Novel in Progress] and giving my feedback where I felt I could, I feel strongly that your work would benefit from a writing coach. You seem to have a fairly strong grasp of the story you wish to tell, and that maybe the mechanics of it all are hindering you a bit. A writing coach can help you get your wonderful imagination on the pages in an organized and aesthetic manner. If you are in need of a referral, please let me know.*

If you struggle to pinpoint the nature of a story's editorial needs—the piece is building toward something, but it still seems awkward to you or just weak overall—that is probably because the piece is not taut; that is, the writing does not all materialize in the desired moment. This is a fine example of a need for a developmental editor. You could say the following:

*I feel you have a fairly good grasp of the story you wish to tell. Your imagination is evident, and you've established a very creative plot. Still, the story is not as tight as it could be. I really think that with some revisions and possibly the help of a developmental editor, you could have the story you envision and one that your readers will greatly appreciate. If you need a referral for a talented and skilled editor, I'd be happy to recommend a few.*

If you've found that the writing has quite a few contextual flaws, grammar issues, punctuation errors, you may want to recommend a copyeditor.

*You've written a compelling story with a solid plot. Your prose is fairly tight, but I spotted multiple areas that included contextual flaws (John's background is inconsistently relayed at various points in the story; the setting has inconsistencies; a few of the characters' names are misspelled from time to time), and there are some significant grammar issues. This is nothing that can't be easily addressed by a skilled and professional copyeditor. Thank goodness for copyeditors, right? If you'd like a recommendation for one, please let me know. I've marked a few of these areas in the manuscript for your convenient review.*

Or maybe their writing is solid and you've only spotted a few typos here and there.

*Your work was a pleasure to read, and you've really got a tight story. As you know, my role is not that of an editor, but I always recommend the services of one. I firmly believe that anything can be improved upon. Most editors offer an evaluation to see if there is anything they can do to make the work even stronger. I recommend contacting one to see what they've got to say. And then of course, if by chance you forego this phase, please do not publish without the services of a professional proofreader.*

*I've highlighted one or two typos—I'm sure there are more—and a professional proofreader will make sure your book looks as professional as it possibly can.*

You could say something to this effect if their handling of prose seems to be the weakness:

*The story you've written is truly creative. I was hooked from the get-go and delighted in the unfolding of it all. I did however struggle frequently with the arrangement of many of the lines. Convoluted sentences and word choices slowed my reading throughout the story. Precision and concise language are the differences between an engaging story and one that struggles with distracting prose. Because I believe you've got such a strong grasp of what you wish to say, I think that simply utilizing a line editor would immensely help to tighten up the prose and get you a truly great book.*

*If you would like a referral for a great line editor, please let me know. And then, of course, I wholeheartedly recommend the use of a professional proofreader before final publication. Along with a few lines I marked for your review to highlight the line editing needs, I've also marked a few typos, spacing errors, etc. There are certainly more, and a professional proofer can assure the most professional book possible in this regard.*

This part of your letter may be the most important. Many self-publishing authors are not aware of the various levels of editing that many successful authors utilize to get those professional-level books produced. The do-it-yourself part of publishing oftentimes leads people to believe that that refers to every step of the process. And it does, to a certain degree. In this sense, it means that the author is personally responsible for acquiring the proper editorial services, not that they themselves are doing the editing. A traditional publisher would provide the editors. A self-publisher must do the same if they wish to produce a professional-level book. So don't fail your authors by skimping on this invaluable information. And of course, make all recommendations with an encouraging, positive, and kind tone.

Your final paragraph will end the letter on a positive note. Recap/highlight their strengths and that you are happy to have had the opportunity to contribute. If you feel they've adequately identified their genre, say so. If you feel there are other keywords to help narrow down the genre, say that too. I always offer my services again, should they wish to utilize another beta read after a rewrite. (Also, I offer my other author services should they need them.) And then of course, I end with something along the lines of *I hope my feedback serves you well, and I wish you and [A Novel in Progress] much success in the future.*

Finally, before finalizing this letter, read it over for the following: 1) areas that are vague, may be unclear, need further explanation; 2) areas where your tone may be interpreted as aggressive; and 3) anything that seems more to refer to them as a writer rather than the work itself.

# SIX
## TACT 101
### *Sometimes It's Not What You Say; It's How You Say It*

I think it is safe to say that, in life, giving and receiving criticism is inevitable. It just is. Like it or not, it is a necessary part of growth. When giving, the challenge comes with the deliverability of that criticism. Poor deliverability of what was intended to be constructive, artistic criticism may result in the receiver blocking any help, or worse, lashing back. Tact plays a huge role in this deliverability game.

**Example of how poor wording of the simplest thing can go south in a hurry:**

**Hubby:** Are you mad?
**Wife:** No. I'm not mad; I'm hurt.
**Hubby:** Hurt? Why? Wasn't what I said true?
**Wife:** It was, but when you word it like that, it feels like you're insulting me.
**Hubby:** Oh, okay. I didn't know. (Here comes the terrible apology, y'all...) I'm sorry you feel that way.

Yikes! We all know what happens next. She is even more pissed than before. All he had to say was "I'm sorry." Or even better, "I'm sorry the way I said that hurt you."

It's all in the framing.

There are many different ways to say the same old thing, but if one of those ways is grounded with tact, its acceptance will have a far greater chance of happening. Let's have us a little crash course on the matter of tact, shall we?

A request for feedback is not a free pass to use your blunt card. Yes, you've been contacted specifically to offer constructive criticism. So they *should* know to expect some negative feedback. So why go to so much trouble to craft it so carefully, as if the author is some delicate and unsuspecting victim? Because that may very well be the case. We don't know exactly what type of feelings this author has around their work and their skills. They may be expecting a glowing response filled with nothing but praise, a confidence boost. They may feel their plot is rock solid and are just awaiting a few minor suggestions on a particular character—and getting feedback about a giant plot hole just may knock the wind outta their sails. We don't truly know their state of mind. Therefore, we must tackle this task as if we could potentially blindside the person. I always write my letter as if I am the receiver and am reading it with little expectations. This way, it helps me to be as objective as possible and to consider their potential interpretation of every sentence I write.

Carefully consider the potential interpretation of your feedback and reframe when necessary. There really is no way to remove all the subjection of a critique. I mean, a book is an artistic creation after all. But there is a way to support our subjective responses with objective (and tactful) reframing.

**Here are some strategies to use:**

**Remove finger pointing.** Finger pointing? In writing? Yes. Direct pronouns like *you* and *your* are the written equivalent of finger pointing and can feel aggressive, putting the author on the defense. Being on the defense sure makes it hard to openly receive anything helpful that may be hidden in that seemingly aggressive message.

*Your plot was poorly written—it was all over the place.*

Obviously "your" is the correct word here. I mean, who else's plot is this? But, since it's attached to a negative bit of feedback, it comes across aggressively. So let's just lighten it up a touch.

*The plot was poorly written—it was all over the place.*

Better, but this is still something I wouldn't appreciate receiving if I was this author.

**Remove emotional triggers.** One of the most important self-edits I perform in my feedback is to review for any potential emotional triggers, particularly negative ones. (I'm not so concerned about the positive.)

"Poorly written" is all this author is going to see—and feel for that matter. This all but says *this book sucked and it took everything I had to read it.* Maybe that's the case, or maybe truthfully there were issues with story structure and organization. But "poorly" is the flashing neon sign here.

So my first order of business would be to reframe this. Let's knock out that judgy word and try to stick with the facts here.

*The plot could use some revisiting—it was all over the place.*

**Reframe negative absolutes.** Remember in *Book 1* we talked about negative absolutes? "The plot was poorly written" has one. It just basically states, point blank, this plot is bad. Reframing to get rid of that emotionally charged "poorly" worked that one out on its own. But what about the second part of the sentence? "It was all over the place" is a negative absolute and needs reframing.

**Show them why they should care.** If you can show the author why this issue is important, why they should care, how it affects the reader, they'll be better positioned to address it effectively. So ask yourself why she should care that the plot was all over the place. How did it affect your reading experience? Reframing in this way serves up the feedback in an easier-to-swallow pill for the author. "I had a difficult time following the overall story arc" is nonaggressive and shows that she should care to fix this because it negatively impacted the reader's ability to follow the story.

*The plot could use some revisiting—I had a difficult time following the overall story arc.*

**Take one for the team.** Remember, the author is on the receiving end of tons of feedback; it's nerve wracking. Why not lighten the load if you can? I do this by shouldering a bit of the burden with the use of "I" and "we." Yes, it's their words and their book, but the feedback is a collaboration. And honestly, it's just my opinion, not a fact, not the dang gospel; so this helps to personalize the message, make it less concrete (negative absolute-ish). Using these personal pronouns redirects some of the focus off of them specifically (less finger pointing), gives a reader's perspective (why they should care), and implies an overall tone of teamwork.

*I had a difficult time following the overall story arc* falls under taking one for the team.

And that's an improvement. It's definitely less aggressive

and a softer approach than that very first attempt. But how revealing is our new statement? Does it help the author? Not yet, since she has no way of knowing what the actual problem is. And it's still not actionable feedback.

**Imbed actionable feedback whenever possible.**

Ask yourself, what was poor about it or what needs work? Why was the story arc difficult to follow? This will require more than that initial one-sentence remark. Most likely, you'll need to craft a paragraph to support this statement, explain your stance. Once you've identified the *why*, you'll be in a better position to offer suggestions for actionable feedback.

**Acknowledge that they already know what to do or what they've done well; you're just weighing in from your experience.**

*I think you've got a creative story here. I love the idea of the killer's biological child being the sleuth. It's not something you read every day and I think your readers will love this concept, this thrilling twist. Here's a thought for you: One of the biggest challenges Mystery writers face is the organization of scenes. One walks a fine line between giving adequate clues and not revealing the mystery too early, and scene organization plays such a huge role in the delivery of these puzzle pieces as well as the flow of the story for the reader. The plot as it stands could use some revisiting, as I had a bit of difficulty following the overall story arc.*

*One of the things that I suggest for my authors to tackle organizational issues is to outline their story arc or plot structure based on what they've already written, not from what they planned to write. Now that you have a completed work, create a new outline. Go scene by scene in your book and write a line or two that defines each scene in a new document. Then go back over this outline and see if you can find where some missing elements are or where some scenes may benefit from a different order. I think when you do this, this outlining of your actual written story, you can get a very clear overall look at what you've got and what may still be in your head that didn't make it to the page.*

*Great work on coming up with a very unique story! I think if you can arrange it so that the reader gets a steady drip of clues, you'll have one heck of a book!*

(If there is a glaring scene out of order or missing or whatnot, you should let them know. This is just giving an example of how to tactfully word that their plot is lacking proper order and completion.)

> **Note: Once you've built rapport and a relationship with an author and gotten to know how they react to feedback, you will find that you may not need all this much "coaxing." You most likely will be able to be a bit more direct, to the point. But until you have established a strong rapport, stick with these methods.**
> **Oh and also, just because you *do* establish that rapport, it doesn't give you a no-need-to-care-about-their-feelings pass. You should always use tact, positive and actionable feedback, and encouragement. If they stuck with you, this is probably one of the main reasons why. So don't veer too far from what's working.**

# SEVEN
## SAMPLE
*Because Sometimes It's Nice to See It Done*

**Note: The novel, names, characters, and all critique was created for purposes of this guide and does not contain any information or words to or from any of the authors I've worked with.**

**EMAIL:**

Good morning John,

Thank you for the opportunity to provide a professional read of *Reaching from the Dark*! I truly appreciate and love getting be a part of this process and hope my feedback helps. I've attached the following for your review:

- Cover Letter
- Professional Read-Through Worksheet
- A PDF of *Reaching from the Dark* with annotations
- A timeline of the story (see letter)
- Author Self-Editing Checklist (see letter)

I'm excited to see your debut novel hit the hands of readers! Please don't hesitate to contact me with questions, for further read-throughs, or other services. I enjoyed working with you, reading your work, and would be thrilled to do so again in the future!

**\*\*\*Please confirm receipt of this email and attached documents\*\*\***

Happy writing,
Dedrie

P.S. Please consider leaving a quick testimonial of my professional beta reading service <u>here</u>. I absolutely love what I do and look for any opportunity to do more of it! Testimonials are key in that regard. Also John, if you know of any writerly friends that are looking for beta reading or proofreading services, a referral from you would be so very appreciated.

Best of luck to you and *Reaching from the Dark*!


**ATTACHED LETTER:**

Hey there John!

Thank you so much for the opportunity to provide a professional read of *Reaching from the Dark*! I am always so excited to dig into a great page-turner and am grateful for the opportunity to be a part of the creative process with you. I know how important it is for you to get this work as close to publish-ready as possible, so I hope my feedback assists in that big feat!

Before I begin, let me just explain a bit of my process with you. I've read *Reaching from the Dark* twice: the first time at my leisure, as with any book; the second time with intention, the professional read-through. I do this so that I can experience the book as a true reader—a true fan of the genre—and offer my subjective opinions, as well as so that I can tackle the book with a discerning eye, one that can offer any and every bit of potentially helpful feedback that I can. It's not an edit, but I do consider every aspect of the elements of fiction in my read-through and will address the strengths and weaknesses (as I perceive them) of the manuscript to show you where my little beta reader senses kicked in.

My ultimate goal is to help my authors. You didn't have any specific requests on the questionnaire for this read, so I approached it as I normally would. I find two read-throughs, an annotated manuscript with comments and questions, a completed worksheet, as well as a letter is the best way to do that.

I spent 5.25 hours with the true read; 4 hours on the professional read; 1 hour on timeline tracking and research (scene with autopsy); and 1 hour for the analysis/letter.

I'm a huge fan of thrillers, especially crime thrillers, and I have an extensive background with the genre, as well as with actual court cases involving medical crimes. (I worked hands-on in the healthcare industry for almost two decades and spent about four years proofreading depositions and trials involving medical cases.) So when I read your book and discovered much of the story revolves around a killer who is also a doctor, my little antennae perked right up! You've definitely written a story that I feel many readers will enjoy—and have managed to make your bad guy relatable, which I personally find fascinating. That's no easy job. Well done!

In the questionnaire that you filled out for me, you listed this novel as a mystery. (By the way, thank you for completing that questionnaire—it makes the read-through a much more thorough and effective process.) My first suggestion is to consider the Thriller and Suspense genre as your main subcategory rather than Mystery when marketing this book. We know who the killer is from early on and spend a great amount of time with him: Dr. Zaborski. I believe that readers will be expecting more of a whodunit if you list this novel as a Mystery. I would consider any of the following categories and subcategories (not exhaustive) when marketing and publishing this novel:

Mystery/Thriller/Suspense > Thrillers & Suspense > Medical

Mystery/Thriller/Suspense > Thrillers & Suspense > Crime > Serial Killers

Mystery/Thriller/Suspense > Thrillers & Suspense > Crime > Murder

Keeping the Thriller genre in mind, I feel *Reaching from the Dark* keeps a consistent macabre tone throughout. Your word choice and theme definitely hold true until the very end. The title itself may be something to reconsider, though. I get a visual of the villain hiding in the dark, secluded, never seen, rather than actually being out and about in the world as Dr. Zaborski is. Just a suggestion to maybe run it by a few other folks, see what comes of it.

I make it a practice to kind of create a timeline for the story arc when I am reading. You'll find in the manuscript small sections of blue highlighting. This is how I tracked it. The story you've created is definitely thrilling, but I found myself a little confused with the timeline. Aside from listing this book in the correct genre, this timeline is probably the most pressing area I feel needs revisiting, specifically in Chapter 18. I actually made a quick little timeline while working, so I've attached that as well for your convenience. Hope it helps.

I felt your characters were spot on, especially Dr. Zaborski. You've done an excellent job with his complex character development, making him someone that I enjoyed spending time with, even though the man is a psychopathic killer. That's so difficult to do, but you've nailed it! My only suggestion for his character actually has to do with his relationship with his wife, Natalie. I felt their relationship seemed slightly forced and affected. There's actually a scene that I commented on to reflect my thoughts on this. (Natalie's character is highlighted in green in your manuscript, by the way.) I'm wondering, if there was a bit more of the two of them, a few more scenes, maybe this would iron this out for the reader. I know I would feel their relationship would seem fully fleshed out if I got just a tad bit more of it. Other than that, the characters you've created are well rounded; they've got clear motivations and limitations; they're interesting and unique.

I typically find that authors spend a bit too much time building up to the hook. Not the case in this work. I think it's exactly where it needs to be and that readers will keep with the story because of how strong this hook is. The opening scene with Dr. Zaborski and the student was chilling and unnerving and grabbed me immediately. I definitely wanted more. You did well to follow with a bit of backstory, but I do think some of it could be held off until later on in the story in more of a drip fashion. The backstory here slowed my reading for a bit too long after that initial hook.

There were nice hooks at the ends of the chapters that kept me wanting to start the next chapter. The only section where my reading slowed had to do with the timeline thing (that I mentioned before). That section also could benefit from a stronger transition into the next chapter, though I feel that if you revisit the timeline and swap a few events, that may straighten itself out on its own. Just be sure to revisit the last of that section and verify that it's got that hook readers have enjoyed so far throughout the rest of your work.

The overall plot was fantastic, scarily plausible, and the pacing was excellent. I didn't find any plot holes, any areas where I got bored, and felt you wrapped it up in the end in a way that was exciting and satisfying. Again, just the timeline and transition in Chapter 18 is the only place I stumbled when reading. There was a contextual bit to revisit in Chapter 7, the autopsy scene. I did a bit of research and included comments to help you clear up one detail that I felt was significant.

I enjoyed the first-person point of view of the story, especially being told from Dr. Zaborski's perspective. But I think it's worth considering a third-person shifting point of view, one that sticks mostly with Dr. Z and Detective Rusk and occasionally follows some of the other central characters: Natalie, as well as some of the victims' families. I, as the reader, was not privy to some of the investigative events other than through Dr. Zaborski's eyes, and that left me feeling a little in the dark in areas where being in the dark did not contribute to the suspense. And I think these events could really bolster some of the other characters. I also wonder if using this third-person narrative could further highlight the binarism between villain and detective, boost their conflict. The first person isn't necessarily not working, in my opinion, but I just wonder if third would give the story deeper conflict.

The dialogue was great. I felt I could pick up the book, read some dialogue, and know by the signature dialect and syntax who was speaking. The tone, voice, and style were on point throughout the entire work. There were a few words here and there that you may want to revisit, as they veered slightly in tone—I've marked them for your convenience in the manuscript. Other than those few instances, great writing style!

Your work was a pleasure to read, and you've really got a tight story. As you know, my role in this read-through was not that of an editor, but I always recommend the services of one. I firmly believe that anything can be improved upon. Most editors offer an evaluation to see if there is anything they can do to make the work even stronger. I recommend contacting one to see what they've got to say. And then of course, if by chance you forego this phase, please do not publish without the services of a professional proofreader. I've highlighted one or two typos, some punctuation issues, some spacing errors, etc. I'm sure there are more (and also realize you are early on in this process), and a professional proofreader will make sure your book looks as polished and professional as it possibly can. I offer these services and would love to work with you again once you are ready for this final phase of the production process.

Overall, you've crafted an excellent book. I believe your strongest asset is the story itself—it's incredibly appealing, creative, and holds a consistent amount of suspense. Your use of imagery, especially when describing the thoughts and feelings of Dr. Zaborski, is exemplary. In fact, I would say it's your strongest writing quality and would be well worth considering the POV switch to third person to see if this strength could be capitalized on with other characters.

I expect this debut novel to be a win for you, John!

Thank you again for sharing your work with me. I look forward to working with you again!

Dedrie


P.S. I've attached a self-editing checklist to help you tackle some of those small but important tweaks I mentioned. Hope you find it useful! Also, if you decide you want a manuscript evaluation by an editor, let me know. I have a few that my authors love to work with.

In this example, I positioned myself as a beta reader and proofreader who has a background in the medical field as well as experience proofreading trials and court depositions. Anytime you can use your past experiences to your advantage, do so. Also, the real me edits and would have stated as much, offering that service if I felt it was needed. In this instance, I couldn't do that, so I recommended the option to refer out for an evaluation. Always do your best to overdeliver. Add as much value to your services as possible with helpful tools, referrals, etc. Your authors will greatly appreciate it!

When emailing this feedback to John, notice that I (in bold) requested a confirmation of receipt. You never want these things hanging out in virtual space—the author thinking you've missed your deadline. Once he replied with a confirmation, I would snail mail John a handwritten thank you card (as outlined in Chapter 6) with an offer to hold a proofreading spot in my schedule with a discount if he signs up and pays within a certain timeframe. When he gives his testimonial, I'll shoot him a thank you email with some other type of value item. Always overdeliver.

I hope this sample helps you get a strong start. I know jumping into anything new can feel daunting, and it always makes me feel better to just watch someone else do it first. Until you hit your stride, feel free to swipe my words and phrases. Use the Professional Read-Through Worksheet to frame your letter, snagging the author's most important strengths and weaknesses to include in the letter. Send the manuscript complete with notes, comments, questions, suggestions, highlighting, etc., but make sure to go back and clean up any potentially harsh, confusing, or aggressive wording before doing so. Once you get the hang of crafting tactful, effective, and well-received feedback, it'll start to flow naturally in your comments and you won't have to do so much editing.

And that's the skinny, folks.

## EIGHT
## FINAL THOUGHTS
*Find Your Mojo, Strut Your Stuff, Love Your Life*

My hope is that from getting a grasp on the fundamentals of fiction from *Book 1*, pairing them with your opinions as you read, and then working diligently to craft your feedback in such a way that is easily received and utilized, your beta reading business will take off. One thing that I learned very early on is that so much of this hinges on how you present your opinions. The packaging matters. It needs to be of good quality, with the author's best interest at the heart of it, and packaged so professionally and beautifully that the author never misses an important point or suggestion due to poor or distracting word choices.

At times I'll find myself thinking, *look, you asked for it. Let me just do us all a favor and make this short and to the point.* But unfortunately, even if an author asks for this, most times they don't really mean it—they're human and struggle to remove personal emotions from the process. Writing a book is just too personal and creative a process to *not* have emotions tied to every aspect of it.

I'm one pretty tough cookie. It takes a bit to ruffle my feathers. I can take a yelling at, some insults even. I mean really, most of the time I just don't care enough to let one person's poor choice of words ruin my day. But I did find that when it comes to discussing my writing, I can get a tiny, little visceral reaction when an unexpected blow comes my way.

I've been writing a Southern Gothic mystery. I meet

weekly with a writing partner. I tell him all the time, no need to pussyfoot around me. Just say what you need to say so I can get this right. And this holds true except in one area: my narrator's voice. I've been told that my register is inconsistent; namely, that some of my word choice (that is sophisticated) does not match the Southern narration elsewhere. I interpret this to be that, since it's Southern, the narration can't use "intelligent" sounding words. I even get a tad offended, truth be told. I'm Southern. I love our little dialect here. But that doesn't mean we don't have a decent vocabulary. *I'm not dumb!* Do you see where I'm going?

My partner is trying to help with narration voice consistency, and I get stuck on this whole dumb Southern stereotype. I know it, yet I can't help it. So even though I've told him to just be blunt, clearly I can't handle it in all areas of my writing. Remember this when crafting your feedback. You can't possibly know an author's buttons. So try your best to steer clear of pushing any. Handle all matters with tact, respect, and care. You'll avoid the author missing the point and focusing on the poor delivery of it. (A quick note: my critique partner did, in fact, state his concern nicely and even offered suggestions. Yet I still felt a slight sting. Keep this in mind. Authors can be extra sensitive.)

One of the best ways to avoid these misunderstandings or potential button-pushing episodes is to call upon Cousin Charisma. She's the woman with class, empathy, creativity, and a knack for tackling the un-fun truths with Southern charm.

## 10 WAYS TO BE LIKE COUSIN CHARISMA

One of the essential tools (and yes, charm and charisma

are tools) used to establish an open and trusting relationship with an author is the magic of charisma. Knowing how to deal with people is helpful for anyone offering services. For the beta reader who relies on written communication, it's paramount. Why? Because charisma helps others see us as a leader, as an authority of our domain, as basically someone who knows her stuff.

It is true that charisma—or knowing just the perfect thing to say in a difficult situation—comes more easily to some than others. We can't all be born Winton Churchills, am I right? But really, tact and charisma boil down this: your morals and values. If you genuinely want to help and encourage a writer to improve their story but are terrified that your inner Awkward Andy may take over when it comes to delivering criticism, fear not. These things can be learned, just like any other valuable skill.

So how do you imbed charm and charisma into something like delivering constructive criticism in written? Glad you asked! Here are ten tips to help you out:

### 1. The sweetest sound in the world is one's own name.

When someone speaks your name to you—unless of course it's your momma and she's used your first, middle, and last name with the old hand-on-hip stance—it shows that you are the focus of their attention. It conveys warmth and genuine interest. When crafting your feedback, especially when giving praise, drop in their name. It will go a long way to give a personal touch. "Rebecca, this line is beautiful! The metaphor works perfectly and does an excellent job of expressing your intended tone. I think if you apply this writing style to the second chapter (where I left a few notes), it would work well."

This goes too for the names of the author's characters. Don't get lazy and refer to "the main character." This author spent a crazy amount of time dreaming up this character. In fact, it probably feels like a real person to her. Use the characters' names, always.

**2. Practice the art of assertiveness.**

With every interaction, whether in the letter, when emailing back and forth during the initial contact phase, or if you end up on the phone or Zooming or in person, convey confidence and decisiveness (this does not mean cocky and aggressive). Confidence in your decision to charge a fee, in your feedback, in your skills—whatever it may be—will send the message of a professional and allow the author to rest a bit easier. An author wants someone who knows their job, their role, and their business. Imagine if you hired a home inspector to assess a potential purchase. He does the job and then when it comes time to deliver the assessment says, "I think your foundation maybe could possibly have some issues...well, what are your thoughts? I would probably do something about it, but you certainly don't have to." Does this sound like someone who knows his stuff? If he isn't confident in his recommendation, would you be? No. Practice and experience help this to come more naturally, but until then, fake it 'til ya make it.

**3. Don't be afraid to show a weakness in yourself.**

I know this seems a bit contradictory to the tip above, but hear me out. Be assertive in general. Be confident in your skills. Gain experience to grow that confidence. But if and when you come across something that you feel unsure about, say so. If 98 percent of your critique is backed with fundamental rationale to support it, couched in a positive and helpful tone, and accompanied with confident action-able suggestions, then that one time you are uncertain of something, just own it.

*John, I'll be honest. I'm uncertain as to how I feel about this scene. My first thought was that Ginger wouldn't do something like that. But then, when I thought about what happened between Edgar and her mom, well, I reconsidered. My gut tells me that it's not working, but I'm not sure as to why. You may want to run this by others to get additional feedback on it.*

This shows that you've put some thought into it, that you don't assume everything you feel is right, and that you just honestly want the best for John's writing. It doesn't reflect as a weakness but rather that you are someone that is self-aware and puts the work first.

### 4. Go the extra mile.

Kindness goes a long way. I've given you access to some helpful templates and resources. Share them with your authors (obviously if it's appropriate). Or if you've come across any book or article or reference you think might be helpful to them, pass it along. Anytime I see a writing contest that's a good fit for one of my authors, I always alert them of it. It's just a nice touch, and it will serve your busi-ness well. I believe in the rule of reciprocity. You give a little upfront, next thing you know, that author will be happy to give back (with more projects, referrals, et cetera).

### 5. Set your intentions before each project.

What's the goal? Why am I doing this? Um...because it's

crazy fun, you love books, and you have been given the coolest opportunity to have a front-row seat to the friggin' storycrafter's party! Remind yourself of these things. Then get busy.

**6. Research shows that how one goes into a conversation determines the result.**

The same can be said for beta reading. Go in looking for a successful book. Point out what works. You'll easily find what doesn't work—we humans are naturally drawn to the negative. But if you go in with an optimistic outlook, you'll have an easier time crafting a letter of constructive criticism rather than a something akin to a giant pink slip.

**7. Be sincere in your compliments.**

Writers become incredibly distrusting when they get compliments they feel they genuinely don't deserve. So doling out false praise is a no-no and will most likely backfire on you anyways. You can avoid this by sticking with truthful affirmations. Affirm the strengths that you have direct evidence of—period.

**8. Master your domain.**

This one takes some time. Actually, as a serial student and lifelong learner, I've learned that it will take forever. That's not at all intimidating, huh? I kid. What I mean is, once you've finished this guide (and hopefully *Book 3* so that you can establish your business and build a wonderful clientele base), don't stop learning. Love Mysteries and plan to market yourself in that niche? Keep learning everything you can about them. Familiarize yourself with the great Mystery writers. Join the MWA. Read as many mysteries as possible in the various subcategories. Study all you can about how writers build suspense. The more you know, the more you've read, the more you'll have in your toolbox. This will carry over as confidence and charisma when interacting with authors.

### 9. Empathize with your sisters and brothers.

Um...what? Haha! I know. Studies show that visualizing others as your family will help your tap into your empathy mindset. It's kind of like when someone says, "Would you kiss your momma with that mouth?" What they mean is, speak to everyone as you would your own mother, with respect. If you happen to dislike your siblings and fear this visualization won't help you, pretend the author is a child, innocent and delicate.

### 10. Be liberal with your gratitude.

I've mentioned that what you appreciate appreciates. And I've recommended including elements of gratitude in the letter you send back with your analysis. So what more is there? A thank you note. In this day and age, people are far too busy, too self-focused and short-sighted to send hand-written thank you notes. If ever you've received one in the mail, I bet you felt a surge of joy. Because it's just so dang rare these days. If you can get a mailing address for your author, I recommend crafting a personal and thoughtful thank you note and mailing it to them. It's a nice touch and you'll stand out as a professional that recognizes this fast-fading charismatic practice. Been a while since you've written and mailed a thank you note? Don't be ashamed. Make the change!

Here's some guidance for you:

- Send it within two weeks of completing the project.
- Send it through the mail. It feels sincerer.
- Use stationery. I suggest buying a pack of nice-looking cards to have on hand.
- Begin by expressing your gratitude for the opportunity to work on [Book Title].
- Mention what you enjoyed about the experience. Be specific.
- Any upcoming news about your business? Any offers or referral incentives? Found something that you think they'd love (like a writing contest or sale on writing software)? Say so.
- Allude to continuing business with them in the future. "I look forward to beta reading your next great mystery!"
- Repeat your gratitude.
- The valediction (the sendoff words you include before your name).
- And then, of course, sign it.

I promise you, if you follow these ten tips for using charisma in your beta reading business, you'll make a positive name for yourself among the self-publishing community. Not all of it may come naturally—we do live in a fast-paced, self-focused world these days—but you can work on them until they do one day become second nature. I hope these tips help bring you an abundance of happy clients and success in this fascinating field!

And that's a wrap, folks! Remember, beta reading is vital for self-publishing authors. Why? Because it is difficult for authors to take an authentic "reader's perspective" on their own stories. Being so close and invested in a work causes author tunnel vision, and what may be obvious to their audience is not so apparent to themselves. The beta reader takes that gap between the two and fills it with helpful, constructive, and encouraging critique.

# NINE
## HELPFUL TEMPLATES
*For You and Your Clients*

Gain access to all available templates and resources by using the following link:

https://tinyurl./BetaReaderBook2Resources

### Self-Editing Checklist

Download this handy self-editing checklist and save it. Use it to create a new one if you like. A checklist to offer your authors may prove valuable someday, especially when you've come across a manuscript that needs a fair share of revision work. My core purpose for getting into this business is to help authors. If I suggest a self-edit because it's not even beta-ready, then I feel I can best help that author by providing a means to assist with that recommended task of self-editing.

### Nondisclosure Agreement

A nondisclosure agreement (NDA) states that you will not share the author's work with anyone. Self-publishing authors sometimes hesitate to give their entire manuscript over for beta reading or editing services. I gladly offer an NDA to put them at ease. Knowing you are not going to steal their story and publish it yourself eases their mind and costs you nothing but a few minutes of your time. Some betas and editors get offended if asked to sign any such thing. It seems silly to get up in arms over one, to me. Just do it, and then you can focus on what really matters: helping the writer get their story as awesome as possible. You're welcome to check out the NDA that I use. I'm no lawyer and cannot advise you in any real way about this matter, so I suggest you check out Rocket Lawyer to gain some insight on legal documents (https://www.rocketlawyer.com/form/non-disclosure-agreement.rl).

## Author Questionnaire for Beta Reading Services

I always send out an author questionnaire so that I'm mighty clear on the author's goals for the beta read as well as the book overall. Here is one I use. There's a download-able logo-free version there as well for your use.

## Project Tracking Worksheet

I am a stickler about tracking my time and adhering to deadlines. You should be too, unless your goal is to rub a whole bunch of folks the wrong way. It may take some practice to form the important habit of tracking your time (you most likely will have many starts and stops), but it will serve as an effective tool for tracking your work efficiency as well as the flow of the manuscript. I like to provide the author an itemized table of my work which also serves to track time spent on the project. I am a big proponent for justifying any work you've done. You're welcome to use the handy-dandy project tracking sheet I use for my beta reads. Hope it helps!

**Character Sketch**

Characters, like real people, have quirks, likes, dislikes, motivations, hang-ups, fears, habits, specific morals, values, and worldviews. A sketch assures that a character evolves while staying true to himself every step of the way. As a reader, if you can't point out how a character evolved throughout the story, you may want to mention this to the author. And of course, you can always send them a character sketch form as an added value and helpful way to address the concern you've raised.

**Professional Read-Through Worksheet**

It's helpful to have a worksheet to follow along or review to assure you consider the many aspects of a novel. Sometimes it's easy to focus on a few areas and neglect others. Here's a worksheet with a list of topics to consider that also can serve as a tool to help you organize your thoughts. You don't have to answer every single question, but it's nice to have a vast list of them handy.

# EXERCISE PART III

By now, you should have a decent grasp on the plot and characters of the book you chose since you've completed a true read (maybe more than once). Using your provided worksheets, fill out what you can and then begin a professional read. You won't have a Word document of this book since it has been published, so you won't be using the Word or iAnnotate tools, but you can still take notes and practice identifying the various elements as you read. Read through all the questions and keep them handy so that you can refer back to them as you go along.

Once finished, practice crafting a letter to see how you feel about crafting feedback. It may come easy; you may find that coming up with ways to word things is more challenging than you anticipated. In any event, put some thought into it and give it a go.

**Note: Most likely, you're not going to find too terribly much that requires suggestions, but you may. Just because something has been published, doesn't mean it's not possible to improve upon it. Just be mindful of the questions and use this exercise to hone your skills for identifying elements.**

# PART III RECAP

In this section you have learned

- how to perform the act of beta reading in an organized and efficient manner
- how to compile the notes, questions, and comments you've made throughout the manuscript
- how to create an effective letter to reflect your analysis, worksheets, marked-up manuscript, etc.
- how to capitalize on tact to craft the most effective and well-received feedback
- ways to incorporate charisma in all your beta reading correspondence
- what a sample email with the letter looks like

And you have been given access to helpful templates and tools to use as you wish in your beta reading business!

## PART III RECOMMENDED READING

*How to Become a Successful Beta Reader Book 3: Establishing
Your Beta Reading Business* by Yours Truly

So, let me just say that I personally have spent thousands of
dollars on university tuition (degree in English and Creative
Writing with a focus in fiction), online courses in editing,
writing, copyediting, proofreading, business creation, business development, social media marketing, author business
courses, and self-publishing courses. I've read countless
books on every one of these topics plus on developing skills
in communication, giving constructive criticism, building

trust, developing professional relationships, confidence, financial management of editorial businesses, etc.

I follow those who are killing it in this industry, including the self-publishing writers themselves. (Man, how I love to see these folks winning!) And I've created an author services business that earns me what I need—I currently beta read, audioproof, write, copyedit, proofread, and offer writing critique/coaching—and no longer work a 9-5 job in healthcare. Oh, let us not forget that I can do this job from anywhere!

The reason I wrote the first two books is because when I set about learning to beta read with greater skill, like figure out exactly what authors were wanting and needing, there was nothing much available other than some blog posts here and there and comments on social media posts. Zilch as far as reference books.

I noticed in social media groups that everyone kind of treats it like a no-brainer. Yet that same everybody complains about unprofessional betas and betas that flake or give vague feedback or how hard it is to find a good beta. I don't believe this is necessarily the fault of beta readers— there are just no standards in place, no resources. So I thought, why not try to create a standard for beta reading? Why not give those who want to learn the skills the foundation to get started off on the right foot, rather than just winging it because they happened to have read a bunch and are fans of certain genres? (With that mentality, I could say, hey, I also eat a bunch, but that doesn't make me educated in the culinary arts, now does it?)

So anyways, my last recommended reading for you in this guide is going to be *Book 3: Establishing Your Beta Reading Business* (https://www.books2read.com/u/mvKD62). Why? Because while knowing the fundamentals of fiction and the

process of beta reading and how to craft feedback is impera-
tive, it is almost pointless if you can't find the clientele to use
them on or manage running an author services business.
Say you want to build a beta reading clientele that starts off
your new quest to build an author services business. You
eventually want to beta read, proofread, maybe help with
marketing or formatting. Whatever it is, you have to start
somewhere; you have to find clients. You have to have a
business platform, have a system in place. You have to know
how to market, how to price, how to manage your author
services business. I can help with that. *Book 3* can help with
that. And even if your goal is to beta read for hobby, for the
pure and simple joy of getting to work with authors on
works before anyone else, you still have to run your services
somewhat like a business—it's just more like a nonprofit!

Whatever your reason, whatever your end goal, give
*Book 3* a read. It'll only bring clarity to a field you are trying
to break into.

## APPENDIX A
*Glossary of Terms*

**Creative writing** is writing that uses the imagination to compose the form and content of a work. This literary term describes a type of writing as opposed to a value judgment such as "that was some impressive imaginative writing." Fiction, in essence, is creative writing (even if not written very creatively).

A **novel** is a work of written fiction. The length varies anywhere from 50,000 to 300,000 words. In the car world, this would be from the Impala on up to a Hummer Limousine ready to haul all the cool cats to the big par-tay.

A **novella** is a work of fiction that is like the Sedan of books. Not quite big enough to hang with the Impala; not quite tiny enough to play with the Mini Cooper.

A **short story** is 1,000 to 30,000 words. Here's your Mini, y'all. Ain't it cute!

A typical manuscript **page** has approximately 250 words.

A **manuscript** is a written or typed document; the original version before publication. Some people like to feel all fancy with this word.

*Curious Kate: "You're a writer? Really? What have you written? Anything I would know?"*

*Fancypants Frank:* "Well, my current manuscript is in its developmental phases at the moment..."

Just call it your book, brah.

**Fiction** is invented prose that causes sleepless nights for those writing (what the hell was I thinking?) and sleepless nights for those who suffer from *justonemorechapteritis*. It's when the beauty of one's imagination fills the pages that bring comfort, excitement, thrill, and pseudo lovers to bibliophiles the world over. Oh, and fiction is usually long and complex and deals with human experiences.

**Prose** is the ordinary language we speak (as opposed to poetry) in the written form. It's sentences and paragraphs, not stanzas.

**Genre** means classification; a broad subdivision of literature. Don't get too terribly hung up on this definition as you will find that all kinds of folks have all kinds of definitions for genre. So here's what I'm going with. There are many genres of writing. Fiction is a genre with many subgenres or categories. The following is a list of fiction categories and subcategories (not comprehensive) as structured by Amazon.

**Literary & Fiction**
Absurdist • Animals • Biographical • Coming-of-Age • Epistolary • Family Life • Family Saga • Genre Fiction • Gothic • Historical • Holidays • Horror • LGBT • Mashups • Medical • Metaphysical & Visionary • Political • Religious & Inspirational • Satire • Sea Stories • Small Town & Rural • Sports • TV, Movie, Video Game Adaptations • Urban Life • War • Westerns

**Mystery, Suspense, & Thriller:**
African-American • Amateur Sleuths • Anthologies • British Detectives • Cozy • Hard-Boiled • Historical • International Mystery & Crime • Police Procedurals • Private Investigators • Reference • Supernatural • Women Sleuths • Crime • Financial • Historical • Legal • Medical • Military • Psychological Thrillers • Spies & Politics • Supernatural • Suspense • Technothrillers

**Romance:**
Action & Adventure • African-American • Anthologies • Clean & Wholesome • Contemporary • Erotica • Fantasy • Gothic • Historical • Holidays • Inspirational • LGBT • Military • Multicultural • New Adult & College • Paranormal • Regency • Romantic Comedy • Romantic Suspense • Science Fiction • Sports • Time Travel • Vampires • Werewolves & Shifters • Western

**Science Fiction & Fantasy:**
Action & Adventure • Alternate History • Anthologies • Arthurian • Coming-of-Age • Dark • Dragons & Mythical Creatures • Epic • Gaslamp • Historical • History & Criticism • Humorous • Magical Realism • Military • Myths & Legends • New Adult & College • Paranormal & Urban • Romantic • Superheroes • Sword & Sorcery • Alien Invasion • Colonization • Cyberpunk • Dystopian • Exploration • First Contact • Galactic Empire • Genetic Engineering • Hard Science Fiction • Postapocalyptic • Short Stories • Space Opera • Steampunk • Time Travel

And then **Teen & Young Adult** have their own full set of subcategories that overlap with many of the above.

The term **abstract** can be used as both a noun and adjective. As a noun, it means basically an outline of the work. As an adjective, it refers to something general and theoretical, something that cannot be described with any of our human senses...unless you're an oracle or something.

**Absurd** means illogical or senseless and can be used artistically to achieve a specific effect. Sometimes authors get all philosophical and dive deep into the absurd...*what are we even here for?*

**Action** are events that occur and are presented through narrative.

An **advance** is money that a publisher pays a writer in anticipation of a completed work. They typically pay in installments: one upon signing and one upon a satisfactory manuscript. Self-publishers don't get any type of advance, but they get to keep the majority of the moolah.

**Adventure** usually refers to books that are all about the fun and events and skimp a bit on theme.

An **agent** is the liaison between the publisher and the writer, the friggin' gatekeeper to publishers (traditional). They work to find placement of the manuscript for the writer taking a fee from the advance and royalties.

An **allegory** is a story that can be interpreted to reveal a hidden meaning. If you've ever read *Animal Farm* by George Orwell, you know that his creation of how life was played out on the farm is representative of the political events of Russia and Communism. In Dr. Seuss's *The Lorax*, the children's tale is entertaining while at the same time serves as straight propaganda against pollution, corporate greed, and excessive consumerism. Allegory = tricksies.

**Ambiguity** refers to having more than one meaning. This can be used on purpose, providing greater depth and meaning (and hella badass book club discussions); it can be accidental, adding vagueness or confusion for the reader (um, *what in tarnation* did I just read?).

**Anachronism** is the act of placing material, events, customs, etc., in the wrong time period or chronological time.

*News of the Black Death swiftly traveled and left London in a state of panic and chaos. People lay dead and dying in the streets, trampled by the petrified. Gerard looked at his wife, beautiful yet decaying before his very eyes, her fingers black with death, neck covered with the tale-tell boils.*

*"Go," she whispered, "Go be with our son."*

*In his moment of pain and fear and disbelief and grief, Gerard kissed his wife on the forehead for the last time*

*"When you find him, please give him this." She handed him her iPod. "Tell him to think of me each time he listens; and that I'll, too, be thinking of him from the heavens."*

Now, this is obviously a bit of an extreme example. But unless you have forgotten your history and the term Black Death did not take you back to the 1300s, a time long before the handy-dandy iPod was invented (or recorded music for that matter!), this passage will not fly.

An **analogy** is a comparison in which one thing is like another thing, usually used to further explain one thing in terms of another. Think *Forrest Grump*: "Life is like a box of chocolates."

An **anecdote** is a brief narrative, typically used to make a point.

*Gerard nodded. He knew this would be his last time to be with his beloved. "It won't be so bad. Our son and I will see you soon, on the other side. Just like the time we got separated from him during the Peasants' Revolt, my dear, we always found our way back to one another. Now sleep, my angel."*

A tad sappy, but you get the idea. He's using a past experience (the anecdote) to assure her the present experience will turn out okay...even though she's rotting before his eyes.

The **antagonist** is the opponent of the protagonist or main character. Remember Annie Wilkes in Stephen King's *Misery*? Yeah, there's one crazy-ass antagonist for ya.

The **anticlimax** is any action that takes place following the climax or resolution, typically disappointing. *Wamp, wamp, waaaa.*

The **antihero** is one that is not stereotypical of a "hero" and is often an ordinary person. I really wish whomever it was that coined this term would have come up with something else, because "antihero" makes me think of the villain or antagonist. Not the case. It's just that the protagonist or hero happens to be not so hero*ish*, just an ordinary dude or dudette.

**Archetype** is fundamental to the human imagination; it is the age-old model by which we understand human experience; it occurs frequently in literature and is an idea, character, or plot. This bit of mumbo-jumbo is based on a Jung premise that all our current emotions stem from those of our ancestors, in a sense. So basically, when we read something with these archetypes—say, a novel that includes a myth about one's search for his father—we, the readers, will instantly have an overwhelming emotional response from the "collective unconscious." Take that and rewind it back!

The **atmosphere** is the prevailing mood of a work.

**Avant-garde** is nontraditional work that is considered innovative or experimental. Ever read *A Clockwork Orange* by Anthony Burgess? Or watched the film adaptation? This work was so nontraditional, so controversial that it has a history of bannings all over the world. If you've not heard of it, it's a dystopian satirical black comedy.

**Beats** are descriptions of physical action that fall between dialogue. Not to be confused with beatings that a character may receive after saying something offensive.

A **bio** (biography) is a brief writing (sentence or short paragraph) about the writer.

*Dedrie Marie is the author of the Pulitzer Prize winning series The Dale, and the story collection Bits of Life. Her stories have been published in The New Yorker, Harpers, and other literary journals. She is also the creator and founder of Lit-Lucrative™, a school that empowers and educates bibliophiles to turn their passion for fiction into careers. She lives in St. Croix and Fort Worth with her Boston terrier.*

(A girl can dream, right?)

**Black humor** is humor that is rooted in morbidity and negativity. Remember *A Clockwork Orange* I was telling you about? Black humor at its darkest.

A **blog** is an online platform with which to build a readership or following. If you didn't know what a blog was before reading this, please email me at lit-lucrative@dedriemarie.com. I would love to meet the person under the rock. I kid.

A **blurb** is the writing on a dust jacket or cover that promotes that book and author or features testimonials. It is not the surprise goo (what the hell is this?) that moms are known to discover in various places: a shoulder, stuck to their chin, acting as cement holding their doctor's appointment card to their current read-in-progress.

A **byline** is the name of the author appearing with a published work. You would see this more in a magazine or news piece.

**Character** can refer to the traits of a person. It is also the label given to the fictitious people featured in a work. The characters are the cast of the book, the supastars!

**Characterization** is the process of developing characters through various literary devices.

**Chronology** refers to the order of events in time.

A **classic** is a literary work that has endured because of its universal appeal. A notable example is *To Kill a Mockingbird*. That sucker was first released in 1960 and still ranks in the top 100 at Amazon in both the Classics and Suspense categories. Can you imagine? *swoon*

A **cliché** is a word or phrase that is overused and unoriginal, resulting in the loss of intended impact. A book filled with clichés is a bad idea and should be avoided like the plague. The writer needs to learn how to think outside the box or risk the book being rejected, ridiculed, and ending up deader than a doornail. But never fear. Every cloud has a silver lining, and *you*, you badass beta reader, will be like a kid in a candy store, taking the tiger by the tail and whipping it into shape. Once you help the author get rid of the lines that serve as nothing but low-hanging fruit, the two of you will be thick as thieves.

A **cliff-hanger** is a plot device used to ensure the reader will keep burning through the pages in a white-knuckle frenzy to see if the work's main character, who has been cleverly placed in precarious dilemmas or confronted with shocking revelations, gets his arse out safe and sound.

The **climax** is the moment of peak development or maximum intensity in a story, the major turning point, the big O...I mean...

**Closure** is the literary resolution, the final salute, the sense of an ending.

**Coherence** refers to the entire work fitting together and being well connected. On the sentence level, it refers mainly to grammar. You know, like you wouldn't have one sentence all poetic and flowery, Toni Morrison style, and then the next super succinct, as to the likes of Hemingway. Overall, it refers to how well a piece "fits together" from beginning to end.

**Colloquialism** is an informal word or phrase used in ordinary conversation. It is key to believable dialogue.

**Comic relief** is what we all need, right? A break from the heaviness of it all with just a dash of funny.

A **comma splice** is a writing error in which two or more independent clauses are joined with a comma rather than a period (and something that is RAMPANT among writers at large). *Here's a fine example of a comma splice, if you write like this you may as well hop your ass to the top of my punctuation shit list.* I kid. Not all are grammar nerds. That's why the gods gave us fine copy editors and proofreaders, right? (Psst, the period goes between "splice" and "if," and since we're at it, I'd throw a comma in after the prepositional phrase "if you write like this.")

In literature, **conflict** is the juicy goodness of the story. It's just what you think it is: characters or forces in opposition. This can be both internal and external, social, psychological (hell yeah), political. Conflict develops drama and suspense and keeps the readers flippin' those pages.

**Connotation** refers to meaning extended beyond words spoken or written. It's what is being implied.

**Context** is the set of facts or circumstances that surround a work and help to determine and clarify its meaning. If the theme is the guts, context would be the—what? Skin?

**Continuity** is a connected series of events that build a plot. It's like the glue. Without it, ya got no flow.

**Conventions**, when discussing genre, it refers to the agreed expectations of the story structure, style, and subject matter that one would find within each genre.

**Co-publishing** (cooperative publishing) is where the publisher and author split the cost of publishing as well as the profits.

**Copyediting** is editing a manuscript for punctuation, context, and grammar.

**Copyright** is a way to protect an author's work from outside reproduction, publishing, selling, or distributing. It's the brand on the cow's hindquarter letting Next Door Farmer Joe know, *this heifer ain't for you*. No breeding, no selling, no chopping up and divvying out to the co-op.

A **counterpoint** can be used to describe simultaneous development of two or more sets of circumstances that have parallel elements.

A **cover letter** is a brief (but sweat-inducing for the author) letter that accompanies work being sent to an editor or literary agent.

In literature **criticism** refers to the evaluation of a work, not like "Uh, this totally sucks" kind of criticism, but an actual analysis using literary theories, etc.

**Denotation** is the literal meaning of a word, sans connotation or hidden meaning.

**Denouement** is when all is revealed and explained in a work, the outcome, the ah-ha moment.

**Description** is narration that reveals what things are like, such as how they look, smell, taste, feel, and sound. Detail in description can bring a flat story to an all-new level when pulled off successfully.

**Dialect** is the way in which language is used in various populations. It encompasses unique characteristics such as phonetics, syntax, morphology, and vocabulary specific to a particular group. Dialect can convey differences in ethnicity, geography, demographics, class, education, and culture. I recently was questioned by my use of the verb "tumped" in my work in progress. I mean, who doesn't know what the hell tumped means? Apparently, folks up North. If you don't know, tumped is Southern for tipped, as in I pushed the upright log until it tumped over onto its side. Then I rolled the dang thang up yonder a bit...for shits and giggles.

**Dialogue** is simply words spoken by characters in a story.

**Diction** refers to the author's chosen words to reflect tone and style. Diction is word choice.

**Didactic** refers to works written to teach or preach. It mostly has a negative connotation attached to the word; so tread lightly if you go describing an author's work this way.

A **double entendre** is a device used to convey a double meaning. Typically, it is used in satirical works. "Marriage is a fine institution, but I'm not ready for an institution." —Mae West

**Empathy**, in literature, refers to when a reader feels what a character feels. This, I believe, is where the true bibliophile is born: out of empathy for our beloved characters. It can also refer to one character expressing or having empathy for another.

**Epigraph** is a quotation at the beginning of a work. It typically is representative of the work's overall theme. That reminds me...let me get on that for this guide.

The **epilogue** is added to a literary work after is has been concluded. It serves to round out the design of the work.

An **epiphany** is a revelation or illuminating discovery, the big ah-ha moment. This happens often for characters caught in a pickle.

An **episode** is a brief event in a longer narrative.

An **epistle** is a formal and literary letter.

**Epistolary** describes novels comprised exclusively of letters. Epistolary novels are stories told through diaries, letters, emails, texts, etc. *Dracula* was one. A contemporary example is *The Perks of Being a Wallflower*.

An **epithet** is a descriptive word added to a name: Dedrie the Facetious. *grin*

An **essay** is a short bit of prose, typically a discussion of some theme or personal thoughts—or possibly even a punishment for acting out in school. "Why I Will Make Wise Choices" by Dedrie Marie.

A **euphemism** is used to purposely obscure the offensive. In the South, when we dole out the old "Well, bless her heart," we aren't actually asking for blessings for the shallow dimwit.

An **exposition** is any definition or explanation of something in writing. Typically, this will come as an interruption of the story to get some background information to the reader.

**Eye dialect** is intentional nonstandard spelling used to reveal more about a character rather than the actual pronunciation of a word and is sometimes used to convey regional or cultural dialectal variations. An example would be using "fella" rather than "fellow." Again, another term that I feel could use some revamping. "Eye dialect" makes me think of some dude giving googly eyes to send a message to the cutie at the end of the bar. This ain't that.

A **fable** is a simple story often making moral points and typically uses animals as characters. Because of this, it fits into the category of fantasy. The fable that comes rushing to my mind to offer as an example is *The Wonderful Wizard of Oz*.

**Fair use** is a provision of the copyright law that says short excerpts from copyrighted works may be used without infringing on the owner's right.

A **fairy tale** is a story involving wonderful and fanciful imaginary and magical characters and is often written (or told, as they sometimes are just stories passed down through the years) for children, though not always. Think

"Rapunzel," "The Princess and the Pea," "Hansel and Gretel."

A **fantasy** involves imaginary characters in imaginary settings, i.e., your escape from reality.

**Feminist criticism** is a means of analyzing a work through the lens of the feminist theory: assumes that female writers and readers have a unique view, attitude, value, and concern —which we totally do, ladies! I'm not one of those "march braless with my picket sign depicting an abstract vagina" kind of gals, but I do strongly believe that women are unique and beautiful and have so much to offer the world through their own brand of passion and creativity. Okay... I'm done. Go ladies! Ahem...now I'm done.

**First person** is the point of view of *I* or *we*. When a book is written in the first person, you are experiencing the events from within the mind of a character. So you get to know their thoughts, feelings, fears, motivations, and opinions about their surroundings and other characters.

A **flashback** is the author's way of illuminating the history of a character or place or event through an interruption of chronological sequence; it is presented as an independent scene often via a memory or reverie.

A **flat character** is one lacking depth and complexity (nothing to do with bra size). Flat is how you would describe a character that is written stereotypically. This is not always a bad thing. It can be useful for carrying out narrative purposes, especially for those characters that do not hold starring roles and the reader doesn't really have to know much about them. They can typically be described using one word or a short phrase: "evil stepmother" or "nosy neighbor." They serve a purpose but do not need their own story arc.

**Folklore** is a body of traditions and legends, typically untrue or unproven, that have been passed down from generation to generation oftentimes from proverbs, myths, work songs, etc. Visit Ireland and you'll get firsthand folklore telling at its finest. One of the best experiences of my life! But if Ireland's not on the radar, you can get some from reading *The Jungle Book* by Rudyard Kipling. It's jam-packed with folklore, and a fun read!

**Foreshadowing** is a literary device used to clue the reader of things to come in a story. Hints, y'all.

**Form** refers to the clearly defined arrangement of the parts in a work, you know, how it's structured. So, like, a sonnet has a traditional form, whereas prose can be highly individualized.

**Format** (in publishing) refers to the physical presentation of a piece, how it looks on the page or e-reader or what have you. There is manuscript format (for consideration by editors and agents) and camera-ready copy or publisher format (refers to the layout seen in a published work).

**Formulas** are often used in writing, such as in detective stories, westerns, romances, and other popular genres. They are conventional ways of developing a story. In this guide, I use the term "conventions" rather than formulas as I expect a writer will spruce them up a bit. It is creative writing after all.

The **front list** is a list of books that are new to the current season. Publishers consider this timeframe to be from the point of publication (woohoo) up to about six months.

**Galleys** are when a work has been typeset but not yet divided into pages. It's the format used (by traditional publishers) for copyediting and proofreading.

A **ghostwriter** is a writer who puts someone else's idea into literary form, not to be confused with a dead dude who continues to write. It is often how writers will "keep the lights on" while plugging away at their own authorpreneurial pursuits.

**Gothic** describes works that contain mysterious, supernatural, and dark elements, such as desolate settings—dungeons, castles, and graveyards—and are often violent, frightening, and strange. Think *Frankenstein*, *The Shining*, *The Shadow of the Wind*.

**Grammar** is the system of rules that defines the structure of a language. It is used to produce and understand sentences, or drive you bat-shit cray-cray if totally botched.

**Hero**, in literature, is the central character, regardless of their qualities.

**Historical criticism** refers to the analysis of a work via the historical criticism theory; that is, attempting to understand the work utilizing what is known of the author and historical period in which it was written.

**Historical linguistics** is the study of how languages change over time. This is something to keep in mind should you find yourself beta reading for a novel set in the 1300s. How we speak has most *def* evolved over time and should be considered, especially in the dialogue.

A **historical novel** is one that uses real characters, settings, and events but with the author's discretion as to the accuracy of such events; often purely fictional stories containing real people and events. A contemporary example would be *The Book Thief* by Markus Zusak set in Germany during the times of the Nazi Regime.

**Homographs** are words that are spelled the same but have different meanings and often different pronunciations. The *content* in this beta reading guide is fantastic! I am *content* with all I am learning.

**Homonyms** are words that sound the same and are spelled the same but have different meanings. I *saw* him pick up the *saw* and *saw* that woman in half!

**Homophones** are words that neither share the same meaning or spelling but sound the same. I, *too*, went *to* the same *two* marked graves looking for the clues, but just as Lester told me, none were *to* be found.

A **hook** is a device or aspect of a piece that catches the attention of the reader and draws them in and makes them yearn for more. Hook = key to establishing an interested reader.

**Imagery** is where words summon up mental pictures for the reader. It draws on the senses, all of them: sight, smell, taste, sound, and feeling. Imagery is the trick to giving the reader an experience and showing them rather than just telling them the story.

**Interior monologue** is the interior thoughts of a character. Just as we real live folks have ongoing conversations in our heads all day long (I hope I'm not alone here), so do our lovely characters. Interior monologue is quite helpful in gaining relatability of a character for the reader.

**Irony** is when the expectation and the outcome of a situation don't quite align.

**Jargon** is used to describe the specialized terminology of an activity, trade, or profession. In this case, you are learning the swanky jargon used among professionals in the literary field. Go you!

A **kill fee** is a fee one receives for stalking, kidnapping, and ultimately—ahem, I mean, for work that was completed, either wholly or impartially, and then canceled. An example would be that a writer sends a manuscript to be edited with an expected due date in two weeks. The editor completes half of the work and then receives an email from the author stating he no longer wishes to complete the service. The editor will then charge a kill fee, which is often included in a deposit.

**Metafiction** is literary work that is about fiction itself and its conventions. It takes some serious skill and brass ones to pull it off successfully. For a fitting example, read *Slaughter-house-Five* by Kurt Vonnegut.

A **metaphor** is a nonliteral comparison of one word or phrase to describe another, a substitution of one idea for another. A metaphor is when you say one thing *is* another. Here's some Southern metaphors, y'all: She's just bein' ugly since she ain't got a pot to piss in. Translation: This woman is financially struggling and therefore lashing out at others in her frustration. But in reality, she's aesthetically accept-able and does, in fact, have one guest bathroom and one master bathroom, both with working toilets.

**Midlist** is the list publishers keep of books not expecting to be best sellers but modest sales.

**Monologue** is speech by one person. So there's no back and forth between characters; you just have one character talking at the other(s).

**Motivation** refers to the conditions that cause the actions of characters. As in life, so do characters have their reasons for their words and actions. Motivations aid character development.

A **myth** is a traditional story (typically of unknown origin) that cannot be logically explained but serves to explain the worldview of a people, a practice, a belief, etc. A contempo-rary example of a book infused with myth is *American Gods* by Neil Gaiman. Mr. Gaiman basically borrowed myths from one end of the world to the other and folded them within his fantasy novel.

**Narration** is the account of a series of events, the telling of the story. The narrator is the one doing the telling.

**Narrative summary** is the portion of prose that is narrated. In literature, it refers to the part of prose where the author is laying out the story for the reader, excluding dialogue and immediate scenes.

**Net royalty** is a payment received from the publisher after all fees have been paid. Ka-ching!

**Omniscient** point of view means all knowing. The teller of the story (the narrator) assumes the all-knowing perspective and relates thoughts, hidden events, and can jump around in time and place.

A **parody** is a humorous imitation of a person, event, idea, or even a society or culture that is intended to be satirical or critical. Seth Grahame-Smith took Jane Austen's *Pride and Prejudice* and created the parody *Pride and Prejudice and Zombies.*

**Pastoral** describes works dealing with simple and rural life.

Writers often use a **pen name**, or a pseudonym, rather than their legal name. Authors will often write under different names when writing in various genres. A great example is Agatha Mary Clarissa Miller Christie (what a mouthful!) known as simply Agatha Christie (aka Queen of Crime). When she opted to try her hand in Romance, she published under the pen name Mary Westmacott.

**Persona** is a narrator created by the author to tell the story, giving distinction between the author's real voice and his/her literary voice.

**Personification** is a literary device used to give human qualities to inanimate objects, animals, or concepts. *The moment her heart surrendered, death collected its prize.* This personifies both the heart and death with the human abilities of surrendering and collecting.

A **platform** encompasses all the efforts made by the author to form a following. This can include a website, blog, speaking engagements, wearing a sandwich board while walking up and down Main Street, and other means of social networking.

**Plot** refers to the arranged series of events in a story.

**POD** means print on demand. This refers to the actual printing portion of the book-making process. You can have books printed in bulk or "on demand" one at a time as needed.

**Point of View** in literature refers to the position or perspective of the narrator, who can either be a participant in a story or just the teller of the story. There are various possible points of view in fiction.

**Proofreading** is close reading and correction of a work's typographical errors.

The **protagonist** is the main character, regardless their qualities (good, bad, etc.). Big Hig is the main character, protagonist, in Peter Heller's *The Dog Stars*.

A **pun** is an amusing play on words. This is *pundoubtedly* a silly example. Ba-dum-bum.

A **query** letter is what an author sends to an agent or editor in an effort to have their work accepted. It is often very brief and includes the author bio and a short synopsis of the work.

**Realism** is an approach to literature depicting ordinary life, regardless how beautiful or wretched it is.

**Register** is the manner of writing style adopted for a particular audience. You would write in an informal register when composing a work of fiction; that is; with a degree of casualness. But that novel may contain a letter written by a scientist addressed to the Center for Disease Control containing his research and articulate opinions regarding the inevitable epidemic to come should the government not heed his warning. This letter would be written in a formal register.

**Resolution** is the outcome of the story, a solution to a problem or resolution of conflict.

**Romance** is a genre involving a love story.

A **round character** (as opposed to a flat one) is a fully developed character that is extremely plausible (fully developed as in fully considered by the author, not round or developed physically).

A **run-on sentence** is a writing error in which two or more independent clauses are joined without punctuation.

A **saga** is a long and detailed account about the adventures of an extraordinary character...or what you call the gossip from one teenage girl to another.

**Sarcasm** is the use of irony or harsh remarks or satirical wit typically directed at an individual but can be an overall tone of a work. *Oh, girl, I couldn't pull that off, but look at you!* Translation: Oh, dear god, what on Earth is she wearing?

**Satire** is a literary device or technique that uses irony, humor, wit, and sarcasm to ridicule or scorn an individual, society, or all of mankind.

A **scene** is a clearly defined unit of action that takes place in real time. A work is made up of many, many scenes. Think of scenes like photos in an album. You flip through the album and each picture contributes its own important piece of the overall story, vacation, childhood, what have you. This is what scenes are in a book.

**Science fiction** makes use of scientific materials but remains within the realm of fiction.

**Second-person** point of view is the viewpoint from the narrator and spoken directly to the audience (you).

**Self-publishing** is when the writer is responsible for all aspects of manufacturing, production, and marketing of the work, including the fees, and keeps *all* the dollars. I refer to the self-publisher as the authorpreneur because he/she's got to basically run an author empire!

**Sentimentality** refers to an excess of exaggerated emotions; can weaken literary work.

The **setting** is the environment and context (place) in which the story occurs.

A **simile** is a comparison of two unlike things typically used to create a nonliteral image. *That Ginger, she's crazy like a fox.*

A **sleuth** is the character in mystery and crime novels that carries out the detective role, though they are not always a professional detective. They are the mystery solver.

The dreaded **slush pile** is the stack of unsolicited or misdirected works sent by authors to agents, editors, and publishers.

**Soliloquy** is speech spoken aloud but representative of the character's thoughts; when a character talks to him/herself.

**Stereotype** refers to simplistic and traditional views, oversimplified and prejudiced attitudes and opinions of something. Think stock characters or actions. Flat characters are often stereotypical.

A **stock character** is one with traditional characteristics but lacking depth or individuality. Think "the evil stepmother" or "the girl next door" or "the mad scientist."

**Stream of consciousness** is a technique used in writing to convey unedited thoughts as they occur. They can appear as incomplete ideas with rough grammar and unique syntax. An excellent example of this is in Toni Morrison's

*Beloved* where she uses this technique throughout the book to allow the readers to get to know the spirit of Beloved.

**Structure** is the form or the blueprint of a work or the plan.

**Style**, in literature, can be that of the writing or that of the editing. When speaking of the author's writing style, it refers to the author's employment of writing techniques: vocabulary used, syntax, imagery, figurative language, and the handling of dialogue and point of view. When speaking of editorial style, I am referring to the standards for the writing and design that are typically established by an organization and followed by publishers and editors.

To **suspend disbelief** is to be willing to ignore one's critical faculties and accept, if for a moment, that fiction is fact in an effort to experience the work fully.

**Suspense** is a literary device used to create anticipation, uncertainty, and anxiety of what is to come. It is also a subgenre of fiction.

A **symbol** is a literary device that uses something specific to represent something more abstract. The ring in *The Lord of the Rings* represents ultimate power, not so much a snazzy piece of bling.

A **synopsis** is a summary of a longer work. When sent with a query letter, it is to be approximately a page to a page and a half and single-spaced. (Always check with agents for specific submission guidelines.)

**Syntax** is the way words are organized into phrases and phrases into larger units (the clause). It's the word order.

**Tags** are used in dialogue to indicate a speaker. The words "he said" is a dialogue tag. Some authors get a bit crazy with dialogue tags. "It drives me nuts when they use these distracting dialogue tags too!" Dedrie growled.

The **theme** is the central idea or overall meaning and impact of the story. It's the heart of the matter.

**Third-person** point of view utilizes a narrator with limited or unlimited knowledge: third person limited or third person omniscient; (he, she, they).

**TOC** is the Table of Contents.

**Tone** is a literary term used to define the feel, mood, and attitude reflected in a work and is achieved through stylistic devices such as word choice manipulation or irony or imagery.

**Translation rights** are sold to a foreign agent or publisher.

An **unsolicited manuscript** is one that was not requested by an editor, agent, or publisher and will mostly likely land smack dab in the slush pile.

**Unity** is a literary quality achieved when all the aspects of a work are cohesive and related by a central theme or concept. It's when all the blood, sweat, and tears of the author's work come together in harmony...and then we all join hands and sway side to side—kidding!

**Voice** is a writer's literary personality and is comprised of a combination of literary devices and stylistic techniques.

**Whodunit** is an informal term (that's super fun to say) to describe a suspense or crime story where the reader continues in search of the answer to "Who committed the crime?"

**YA** stands for Young Adult, or if you're unread, it could just mean "you." As in "Ya want to grow some brains? Read a book, sister!"

So there you have it: my version of a glossary. I hope my spin on defining and explaining the terms will resonate and stick with you. If not, I blame you for not having a sense of glossarial adventure. Ha! Glossarial—how's *that* for a bonus word!

**Abstract:** meaning theoretical or vague
**Absurd:** illogical; ridiculous; silly; implausible; foolish
**Accusatory:** suggesting someone has done something wrong; complaining
**Acerbic:** sharp; forthright; biting; hurtful; abrasive; severe
**Admiring:** approving; think highly of; respectful; praising
**Aggressive:** hostile; determined; forceful; argumentative
**Aggrieved:** indignant; annoyed; offended; disgruntled
**Ambiguous:** having multiple potential meanings
**Ambivalent:** having mixed feelings; uncertain; in a dilemma; undecided
**Amused:** entertained; diverted; pleased
**Analytical:** inclined to examine things by studying their contents or parts
**Anecdotal:** involving short narratives of interesting events
**Angry:** resentful; enraged
**Animated:** full of life or excitement; lively; spirited; impassioned; vibrant
**Apathetic:** showing little interest; lacking concern; indifferent; unemotional
**Apologetic:** full of regret; repentant; remorseful; acknowledging failure
**Appreciative:** grateful; thankful; showing pleasure
**Ardent:** enthusiastic; passionate
**Arrogant:** pompous; disdainful; overbearing; condescending; vain; scoffing

**Assertive:** self-confident; strong willed; authoritative; insistent

**Articulate:** able to express your thoughts, arguments, and ideas clearly and effectively; writing or speech is clear and easy to understand

**Austere:** stern; strict; frugal; unornamented

**Awestruck:** amazed; filled with wonder/awe; reverential

**Belligerent:** hostile; aggressive; combatant

**Benevolent:** sympathetic; tolerant; generous; caring; well meaning

**Bitter:** angry; acrimonious; antagonistic; spiteful; nasty

**Bland:** undisturbing; unemotional; uninteresting

**Boring:** dull; tedious; tiresome

**Callous:** cruel disregard; unfeeling; uncaring; indifferent; ruthless

**Candid:** truthful; straightforward; honest; unreserved

**Caustic:** biting; corrosive; abrasive; critical

**Cautionary:** gives warning; raises awareness; reminding

**Celebratory:** praising; pay tribute to; glorify; honor

**Chatty:** informal; lively; conversational; familiar

**Cinematic:** having the qualities of a motion picture

**Circuitous:** taking a long time to say what you really mean when you are talking or writing about something; not being forthright or direct

**Classical:** formal; enduring; standard; adhering to certain traditional methods

**Clean:** unoffensive language, especially because it does not involve sex

**Colloquial:** characteristic or ordinary and informal conversation

**Comic:** humorous; witty; entertaining; diverting

**Compassionate:** sympathetic; empathetic; warm-hearted; tolerant; kind

**Complex:** having many varying characteristics; complicated

**Compliant:** agree or obey rules; acquiescent; flexible; submissive

**Concerned:** worried; anxious; apprehensive

**Conciliatory:** intended to placate or pacify; appeasing

**Concise:** using very few words to express a great deal

**Condescending:** having a superior attitude; patronizing

**Confessional:** characterized by personal admissions of faults; used more recently to describe very personal, autobiographical writing

**Confused:** unable to think clearly; bewildered; vague

**Contemptuous:** expressing contempt or disdain

**Conventional:** ordinary; usual; conforming to established standards

**Conversational:** informal, like a private conversation

**Cool:** unaffected by emotions, especially anger or fear

**Crisp:** clear and effective

**Critical:** finding fault; disapproving; scathing; criticizing

**Cruel:** causing pain and suffering; unkind; spiteful; severe

**Curious:** wanting to find out more; inquisitive; questioning

**Cynical:** a tendency to believe that all human behavior is selfish and opportunistic

**Decadent:** marked by a decay in morals, values, and artistic standards

**Declamatory:** expressing feelings or opinions with great force

**Defensive:** defending a position; shielding; guarding; watchful

**Defiant:** obstinate; argumentative; contentious

**Demeaning:** disrespectful; undignified

**Depressing:** sad; melancholic; discouraging; pessimistic

**Derivative:** coming from something or someone else (as in the style of another writer)

**Detached:** aloof; objective; unfeeling; distant

**Diffuse:** wordy; difficult to understand

**Dignified:** serious; respectful; formal; proper

**Diplomatic:** tactful; subtle; sensitive; thoughtful

**Disapproving:** displeased; critical; condemnatory

**Discursive:** including information that is not relevant to the main subject

**Disheartening:** discouraging; demoralizing; undermining; depressing

**Disparaging:** dismissive; critical; scornful

**Direct:** straightforward; honest

**Disappointed:** discouraged; unhappy because something has gone wrong

**Dispassionate:** impartial; indifferent; unsentimental; cold; unsympathetic

**Distressing:** heart-breaking; sad; troubling

**Docile:** compliant; submissive; deferential; accommodating

**Dreamlike:** having the characteristics of a dream

**Dreary:** depressing; dismal; boring

**Earnest:** showing deep sincerity or feeling; serious

**Earthy:** realistic; rustic; coarse; unrefined; instinctive; animal-like

**Economical:** efficient with words

**Egotistical:** self-absorbed; selfish; conceited; boastful

**Elegiac:** expressing sorrow or lamentation

**Elliptical:** obscure; suggesting what you mean rather than saying or writing it clearly

**Eloquent:** expressing what you mean using clear and effective language

**Empathetic:** understanding; kind; sensitive

**Emphatic:** using emphasis or boldness in speech or writing, or action

**Encouraging:** optimistic; supportive

**Enthusiastic:** excited; energetic

**Epigrammatical:** a tendency to make use of epigrams, which are terse, witty, or pointed sayings

**Epistolary:** relating to the writing of letters

**Euphemistic:** softened, indirect, innocuous expressions are used for talking about unpleasant or embarrassing subjects without mentioning the things themselves

**Evasive:** ambiguous; cryptic; unclear

**Evocative:** having the ability to call forth memories or other responses

**Excited:** emotionally aroused; stirred

**Experimental:** inclined to try out new techniques or ideas

**Facetious:** inappropriate; flippant

**Farcical:** ludicrous; absurd; mocking; humorous and highly improbable

**Fashionable:** comforting to whatever the current fashion is in language, manners, and/or literature

**Fatalistic:** believing that everything that happens is destined, and therefore, out of the hands of the individual

**Flamboyant:** conspicuously colorful or bold

**Flippant:** superficial; glib; shallow; thoughtless; frivolous

**Flowery:** the use of complicated words that are intended to make it more attractive

**Fluent:** expressing yourself in a clear and confident way, without great effort

**Forceful:** powerful; energetic; confident; assertive

**Formal:** respectful; stilted; factual; following accepted styles/rules

**Frank:** honest; direct; plain; matter-of-fact

**Frustrated:** annoyed; discouraged

**Gentle:** kind; considerate; mild; soft

**Ghoulish:** delighting in the revolting or the loathsome

**Gimmicky:** tricky, sometimes excessively, as in contrived endings

**Grandiloquent:** pompous; haughty; expressed in extremely formal language to impress people, and often sounding overbearing or silly because of this

**Grim:** serious; gloomy; depressing; lacking humor; macabre

**Gullible:** naïve; innocent; ignorant

**Hard:** unfeeling; hard-hearted; unyielding

**Heavy:** profound or serious

**Heroic:** bold; altruistic; like a hero

**Humble:** deferential; modest

**Humorous:** amusing; entertaining; playful

**Hypercritical:** unreasonably critical; hair splitting; nitpicking

**Hysterical:** uncontrollably or violently emotional, whether with fear or rage or laughter

**Idiomatic:** expressing things in a way that sounds natural

**Impartial:** unbiased; neutral; objective

**Impassioned:** filled with emotion; ardent

**Imploring:** pleading; begging

**Impressionable:** trusting; child-like

**Inane:** silly; foolish; stupid; nonsensical

**Inarticulate:** not able to express clearly what you want to say; not spoken or pronounced clearly

**Incensed:** enraged; riled; exasperated

**Incoherent:** without logical connections; difficult to understand

**Incredulous:** disbelieving; unconvinced; questioning; suspicious

**Indignant:** annoyed; angry; dissatisfied

**Informal:** usually referring to register; used about language or behavior that is suitable for using with friends but not in formal situations

**Informative:** instructive; factual; educational

**Inspirational:** encouraging; reassuring

**Intense:** earnest; passionate; concentrated; deeply felt

**Intimate:** familiar; informal; confidential; confessional

**Ironic:** characterized by an unexpected turn of events; often the opposite of what was intended

**Irreverent:** showing disrespect for things that are usually respected or revered

**Jaded:** bored; having had too much of the same thing; lacks enthusiasm

**Joyful:** positive; optimistic; cheerful; elated

**Journalistic:** characterized by the kind of language usually used in journalism

**Judgmental:** critical; finding fault; disparaging

**Juvenile:** immature or childish (can be a fault as in with adults, or meaning intended for children)

**Laudatory:** praising; recommending

**Learned:** a learned piece of writing shows vast knowledge about a subject, especially an academic subject

**Light-hearted:** carefree; relaxed; chatty; humorous

**Literary:** involving books or the activity of writing, reading, or studying books; relating to the kind of words that are used only in stories or poems, and not in normal writing or speech; a form of writing with the goal of producing art rather than entertainment for the masses

**Loving:** affectionate; showing intense, deep concern

Lyrical: intense; spontaneous; musical

**Macabre:** gruesome; horrifying; frightening

**Malicious:** desiring to harm others or to see others suffer; ill-willed; spiteful

**Mean-spirited:** inconsiderate; unsympathetic

**Melodramatic:** having the characteristics of melodrama, in which emotions and plot are exaggerated and characterization is shallow

**Metaphorical:** making use of metaphors, which are figures of speech; nonliteral comparisons

**Metaphysical:** preoccupied with abstract things, especially the ultimate nature of existence and reality

**Minimalist:** inclined to use as few words and details as possible

**Mocking:** scornful; ridiculing; making fun of someone

**Monotonous:** tiresome or dull because of lack of variety

**Mournful:** feeling or expressing grief

**Mystical:** having spiritual or occult qualities or believing in such things

**Naïve:** innocent; unsophisticated; immature

**Narcissistic:** self-admiring; selfish; boastful; self-pitying

**Nasty:** unpleasant; unkind; disagreeable; abusive

**Negative:** unhappy; pessimistic

**Nostalgic:** inclined to long for or dwell on things of the past

**Objective:** uninfluenced by personal feeling; seeing things from the outside, not subjectively

**Obscure:** unclear; indistinct; hard to understand

**Obsequious:** overly obedient and/or submissive; fawning; groveling

**Ominous:** indicating or threatening evil or danger, as dark clouds indicate that a storm is coming

**Optimistic:** hopeful; cheerful

**Ornate:** using unusual words and complicated sentences

**Orotund:** containing extremely formal and complicated language intended to impress people

**Outraged:** angered and resentful; furious; extremely angered

**Outspoken:** frank; candid; spoken without reserve

**Parenthetical:** not directly connected with what you are

saying or writing

**Parody:** a satirical imitation of something serious

**Pathetic:** expressing pity, sympathy, tenderness

**Patronizing:** condescending; scornful; pompous

**Pejorative:** expresses criticism or a bad opinion of someone or something

**Pensive:** reflective; introspective; philosophical; contemplative

**Persuasive:** convincing; influential; plausible

**Pessimistic:** seeing the negative side of things

**Philosophical:** interested in the study of the basic truths of existence and reality; inclined to have a calm and accepting attitude toward the realities of life

**Picturesque:** unusual; interesting; striking

**Pithy:** short and effective

**Playful:** full of fun and good spirits; humorous; jesting

**Poetical:** having the qualities of poetry, such as pleasing rhythms or images

**Polemical:** involving a controversial argument or disputation

**Political:** involved in politics; contains characteristics of propaganda

**Pompous:** displaying one's importance in an exaggerated way

**Ponderous:** serious; weighty; laborious; boring

**Portentous:** trying to seem very serious and important to impress people

**Pragmatic:** preferring practical action and consequences to theory and abstractions

**Precious:** being affected in matters of refinement and manners, sometimes ridiculously so

**Pretentious:** having and displaying an exaggerated view of one's own importance

**Profound:** insightful; deep

**Prolix:** verbose; long-winded; rambling

**Psychological:** having to do with human mind and human behavior

**Punchy:** terse; clear; effective; succinct

**Puritanical:** strict or severe in matters of morality

**Rambling:** long, wordy, and confusing

**Readable:** clear and able to be read

**Realistic:** accurate; authentic; inclined to represent things as they really are

**Regretful:** apologetic; remorseful

**Repetitious:** tediously repeating the same thing

**Resentful:** aggrieved; offended; displeased; bitter

**Resigned:** accepting; unhappy

**Restrained:** controlled; quiet; unemotional

**Reverent:** showing deep respect and esteem

**Righteous:** morally right and just; guiltless; pious; god-fearing

**Rhetorical:** communicating through writing with literary devices and compositional techniques; sometimes thought contrived or pretentious

**Rhythmic:** characterized by certain patterns, beats, or accents

**Romantic:** having feelings or thoughts of love; when associated with nineteenth-century literature or any such literature, it suggests a style that emphasizes freedom of form, imagination, and emotion

**Rough:** incomplete

**Roundly:** complete; in a strong and clear way

**Sarcastic:** inclined to use nasty or cutting remarks that can hurt people's feelings

**Sardonic:** mocking; taunting; bitter; scornful; sarcastic

**Satirical:** using sarcasm and irony, often humorously, to expose human folly

**Scathing:** critical; stinging; unsparing; harsh

**Scornful:** expressing contempt or derision; scathing; dismissive

**Sensationalistic:** provocative; inaccurate; distasteful

**Sensuous:** taking pleasure in things that appeal to the senses

**Sententious:** expressing opinions about right and wrong behavior in a way that is intended to impress people

**Sentimental:** expressing tender feelings, sometimes excessively, hence the phrase "sloppy sentimentality"

**Shakespearean:** using words in the way that is typical of Shakespeare's writing

**Sharp:** precise; biting; harsh

**Sincere:** honest; truthful; earnest

**Skeptical:** disbelieving; unconvinced; doubting

**Solemn:** not funny; in earnest; serious

**Sophisticated:** worldly and experienced; intricate or complex. In writing, a sophisticated style may suggest complexity or considerable experience in the craft.

**Stark:** plain; harsh; simple; bare; bleak; grim

**Stilted:** very formal, sometimes excessively, as in stilted prose

**Stylistic:** relating to ways of creating effects, especially in language and literature

**Subjective:** relying on one's own inner impressions, as opposed to being objective

**Submissive:** compliant; passive; accommodating; obedient

**Subtle:** delicate in meaning, sometimes elusively so

**Succinct:** expressed in a very short but clear way

**Sulking:** bad-tempered; grumpy; resentful; sullen

**Superficial:** shallow; trivial; dealing only with the surface of things

**Surrealistic:** stressing imagery and the subconscious; sometimes distorting ordinary ideas to arrive at artistic truths

**Symbolic:** using material objects to represent abstract or complex ideas or feelings

**Sympathetic:** compassionate; understanding of how someone feels

**Thoughtful:** reflective; serious; absorbed

**Tolerant:** open-minded; charitable; patient; sympathetic; lenient

**Tragic:** disastrous; calamitous

**Trite:** stale; worn out

**Turgid:** complicated and difficult to understand

**Unassuming:** modest; self-effacing; restrained

**Uneasy:** worried; uncomfortable; edgy; nervous

**Unprintable:** used for describing writing or words that you think are offensive

**Urbane:** sophisticated; socially polished

**Urgent:** insistent; saying something must be done soon

**Vague:** unclear; indefinite; imprecise; ambiguous

**Venomous:** poisonous; malicious

**Verbose:** using more words than necessary

**Vindictive:** vengeful; spiteful; bitter; unforgiving

**Virtuous:** lawful; righteous; moral; upstanding

**Well-turned:** expressed well

**Whimsical:** inclined to be playful, humorous, or fanciful

**Witty:** being able to perceive and express ideas and situations in a clever and amusing way

**Wonder:** awestruck; admiring; fascinating

**Wordy:** using more words than necessary to say what you have to say

**World-weary:** bored; cynical; tired

**Worried:** anxious; stressed; fearful

**Wretched:** miserable; despairing; sorrowful; distressed

# ABOUT THE AUTHOR

~

"I always come to life after coming to books"

— JORGE LUIS BORGES

I'm Dedrie and I've created Lit-Lucrative™—a budding e-school created to teach and embolden those wanting to enrich their lives with the wonderful world of books—to help fuel a passion I have for literature and the art of writing and reading with a purpose. This passion of mine started at an early age. At seven years old, I was interviewed on a stage (I was a pageant brat in the South) and asked what I wanted to be when I grew up. My response: a writer and a tap dancer. Lofty!

I do both. I do not earn any income from tap dancing (goals!), but I certainly love it. And I did not always earn an income writing or working with words. In fact, once I hit the age where I needed to get serious about the "What do you want to be?" question, I was of the mind that I could not do what I loved *and* merit a reasonable living doing it. Somewhere along the way I became stifled in my ambitions. So I just chose a fine-enough career and went for it.

For almost two decades I worked in healthcare in some capacity or another and enjoyed parts of it. But I felt stuck. It certainly didn't feel like I was doing anything I was passionate about—I had the typical American work week/work year where I busted my butt all year for a measly week or two of vacation, only to return knowing I wouldn't be able to do it again for another year. I had an overall sense of unfulfillment and felt mired in a passionless job. So I took some time to evaluate my life.

I contemplated all that I love and what my perfect life would look like, had I the choice. I considered my happiness, my goals, my physical health, my emotional health, and my financial health. I considered the balance, or lack thereof, in my life, observing the teetering of work and rest, work and play, and its constant battle to sink me. Fulfilling activities that surfaced over and over were reading and writing and traveling. *Does reading and writing make me happy? Yes. Does it contribute to my overall sense of well-being? Yes. How does it affect my financial health? Well, other than frequent trips to the bookstore denting my pocketbook, I don't know. Hmm.* This gave me something to meditate on. And meditate, I did.

I decided that I wanted to somehow earn a living in the literary world and be able to do so from anywhere I chose. But how? A career in the literary field felt foreign and beyond reach. And what were the options even? I had an education, but it was in healthcare.

I deduced that I obviously had to start all over. And at thirty-something, I did. I went back to college and enrolled in the English and Creative Writing (with a focus in fiction) program at Southern New Hampshire University. I also enrolled in every online editorial, publishing, writing, business development, and marketing course I could afford (aka charge to a credit card). Let me tell you, I've been one busy girl!

While working full-time, going to school for creative writing, taking online courses in editing, copyediting, proofreading, business creation and development, and authorpreneurship, I decided to start an editorial business. In addition, I read countless books, listened to numerous podcasts, sat through way too many webinars, and searched through hundreds of blogs and online articles to gain as much knowledge as possible. I attended as many author events as possible, learning firsthand what successful (even award-winning) published authors find crucial to their success. (Beta readers are high on the list!)

I cannot tell you how much knowledge I've scooped up over the past years just researching this. But what I **can** tell you is that much of what I spent time on could have easily been condensed. I would have loved to have found a course (that wasn't years of time and tuition...arm and a leg) or book that was that one-stop shop when it came to getting all my ducks in a row for a career in this field. And I had the hardest time finding any resources specifically for beta reading. So I decided to create one just for you!

At the time of this writing, I am still attending university. I can't help it; I love it! I am still educating myself as much as possible in the art of writing. I am still reading, reading, reading. But I've decided that I would feel absolutely giddy and honored to be able to share all I have learned with you and what has worked for me in my business. I would love nothing more than for you to read this book, love it, learn from it, earn from it, and then shout to the world that you have a new skill set that you love and can do anytime, anywhere.

And so that is my mission. I do not guarantee that beta reading is for everyone, but I do know that striving to learn something new or to improve in any way can do nothing but good for the soul. I love that I get to do something I love and am rewarded for it. My wish is the same for you.

Fellow book lover, it was a pleasure to introduce myself to you. I certainly hope you find this book valuable and love beta reading as much as I do!

# NOTES

Now, if I were you, my lil' antennae would have tingled when I talked about beta readers working for free, quid pro quo, or a fee. I personally don't work for free. I understand some have an interest in having a hobby that they excel in. I get it. But for those who want to earn from this very valuable skill set, this skill set that authors seek out more often than not, beta reading can be offered as a paid service. There are plenty of folks who beta for a fee—just Google "beta reading service."

I'm not a dime-a-dozen commodity; nor do you have to be. So whether we are talking about working on select hobby projects or tons of paying gigs, this series has the answers to getting you those irresistible qualities, skills, and practices that all the authors will shout to the rooftops about. This series will also help you keep a pulse on your confidence levels, because having the skills is just one-half of the equation; you have to have the confidence to be able to put those valuable skills to work. That's why I incorporated a thing or two about confidence: the science behind it, walking the walk, and taking control of your new bookish venture. Being the newbie in an unfamiliar world can feel like showing up to the junior high lunch room holding a sad saggy paper sack without a friend in sight. So I'll be your friend. I'll guide you until you find your place and voice and confidence to tackle your new beta reading life. (I'm so excited for you already!) And if you feel you'd like more guidance than what's in this series, you should look into the free video training or the premium training. (see additional resources)

The thing I struggled with most having a 9-5 job was the dreaded time-off requests. Something about having to ask permission to spend time with my friends and family never settled with me. I had a decent job working in healthcare—I love to help others—but what I love more is freedom (and freedom opens doors to many ways to help folks). The companies I worked for would (almost) always approve the requests, but it came with the knowledge that I'd have to make up those patient visits when I returned. Not really much of a holiday.

The most precious thing working with authors (and writing my own books) has given me is freedom. I work hard —not that it feels like work—but it's on my terms. And I haven't had to submit a time-off request to my *new* boss...well, ever.

Also, if getting rich is what you're after, let me be candid —you're not gonna get monetarily rich with beta reading. You *can* earn while you read. So if a supplemental income would help out, go for it. Become a beta reader and be that subtle voice that helps an author become a best seller. Want even more ways to earn while reading? Consider copyediting, proofreading, book formatting, cover designing—there are so many ways. You absolutely can earn a living with one or two editorial skill sets.

As a beta, more than anything you'll be enriched by the work itself. If ever I was stranded on an island with only one wish, it would be to have all the books. Books enrich our lives unlike anything else on Earth. They are food for the soul, the mind, the heart. Love can be found lingering between the lines; a mystery can hide in the shadows beneath the cover; an adventure can race you from one page to the next. I just think it's pretty cool to be a part of the success of a book. If you'd like to learn even more about the fascinating gig of beta reading, check out *How to Become a Successful Beta Reader Book 3: Establishing Your Beta Reading Business (https://www.books2read.com/u/mvKD62).* I think you'll love it.

# ADDITIONAL RESOURCES

∿

IF YOU'D LIKE MORE HELP IN YOUR JOURNEY TO BECOMING A
SUCCESSFUL BETA READER, THE FOLLOWING RESOURCES ARE
AVAILABLE TO YOU:

You've just read the second book in a three-book series. In case you missed the first one, *How to Become a Successful Beta Reader Book 1: Learning the Fundamentals of Fiction*, you might want to snag a copy. It teaches you the essential foundational elements that you are reading for when performing a beta read. Pretty important stuff!

Click HERE for *Book 1* or find it at

https://www.books2read.com/u/mZP7Xe

*How to Become a Successful Beta Reader Book 3: Establishing Your Beta Reading Business* will go deeper into the fun and fascinating world of working with authors and the stories they create. You'll learn the ins and outs of establishing, marketing, and growing your beta reading business.

Click HERE for *Book 3* or find it at

https://www.books2read.com/u/mvKD62

Want a comprehensive step-by-step course to take you from scratch to established? BECOMING LIT-LUCRATIVE: Beta Reading is a multi-media online course made for anyone looking to get their foot in the door as an author services provider starting with beta reading.

Enroll HERE for online courses

or visit www.DedrieMarie.com/lit-u.

I share useful links and tips. Connect with me:

(f) www.facebook.com/dedriereads

(p) www.pinterest.com/dedriemarie

(w) www.dedriemarie.com

(t) www.twitter.com/dedriemarie

**More books and courses by Dedrie Marie:**

**Fiction Books in Progress:** Southern Gothic Mystery (written under Bebo Franklin)

*Elemdale Book 1*

*Elemdale Book 2*

*Elemdale Book 3*

You can sign up to be notified of new releases, giveaways, and pre-release specials—plus get a free short story from Bebo Franklin!

**Courses:**

COMMA SUTRA: Proofreading Fiction

# DEAR READER

~

I'd love to get your honest feedback on this book. My aim is to share the knowledge I've gained. I think it's our duty as fellow humans. But I don't claim to be an expert, just a lover of the craft.

If you have any comments or questions about the information here, shoot me an email at lit-lucrative@dedriemarie.com. I'd love to hear from you.

And of course, don't forget to **leave a review**—again, an honest one. Reviews help others make an informed decision about taking a chance on a book. They also are vital to the success of an author's career. So PRETTY PLEASE leave one.

You can leave a review with the retailer from which you purchased this book. Also, any reviews left on my Goodreads page would be greatly appreciated!

https://www.goodreads.com/book/show/42090135-how-to-become-a-successful-beta-reader-book-2/dedriemarie

Thank you for the courtesy of reading this book. I hope you've found it helpful in some way.

Happy reading,
  *Dedrie*

# THE OBLIGATORY DISCLAIMER

While every effort has been made to accurately represent how to identify and use the fundamentals of fiction and recommended tools and systems to beta read for self-publishing authors for free, quid pro quo, or a fee, there is no guarantee that you will earn any money. Any person or product that tells you otherwise is fibbing—as nothing in life is guaranteed.

There are affiliate links within this book to products and services that I personally use and recommend. This means I receive a small percentage of sales with no extra cost to you; and in some cases, you may receive a discount for using my links. I only recommend services that I personally use and believe are great for doing this work! If you're wondering why I recommend author services for you, the beta reader, it's because at some point your author will ask for advice. Wouldn't it be great if you could point them in the right direction? Going above and beyond to help your clients is THE BEST way to keep them and maybe get a few word-of-mouth referrals from them. It's a win-win.

**FREE VIDEO TRAINING**

Get the system I use to make my reading habit work for me:

www.DedrieMarie.com/start-beta-reading

Hope to see you there!

*Dedrie Marie*

Made in the USA
Columbia, SC
26 July 2022